SEKIRO
SHADOWS DIE TWICE
Official Artworks

隻狼

THE ONE-ARMED WOLF, A SHADOW IN THE SENGOKU PERIOD.

SEKIRO™
SHADOWS DIE TWICE
Official Artworks

TABLE OF CONTENTS

I ◆ IMAGE BOARDS

In the Sengoku period, blood was washed with blood. Burning skies, nights choked with smoke—these images bring to life the ominous, inhuman land of Ashina.

This book is a collection of artworks from the action-adventure game *Sekiro: Shadows Die Twice*, developed by FromSoftware, published by Activision, and released on March 22, 2019. In this book, you will find everything from story-related image boards to character designs, concept designs for items, and other important parts of the game world. All aspects of the art selection and book layout were overseen by FromSoftware, and we have worked hard to show the world's style as best as we could.

Sekiro presents a unique vision of the Sengoku period, with bloody, twisted battlefields alongside colorful scenes of ancient Japan. We hope this book will lead you to ponder this contrast in *Sekiro*'s deep yet fanciful world.

Daisuke Kihara,
Dengeki Game Books
Editorial Department

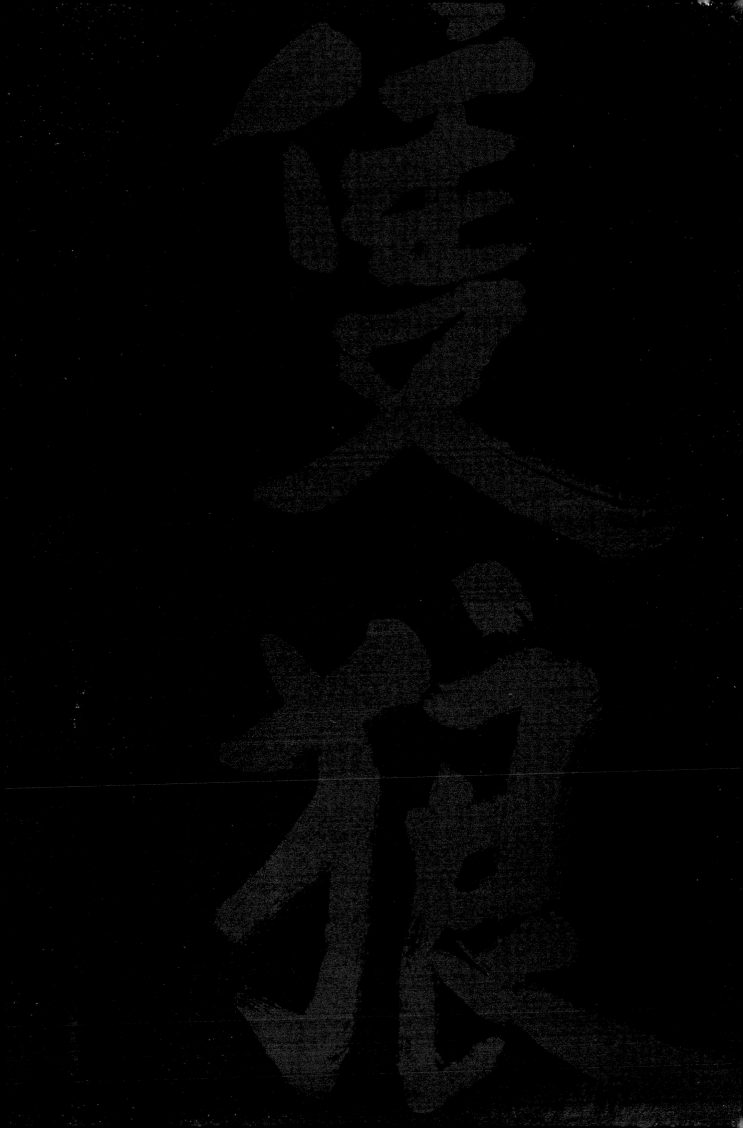

IMAGE
BOARDS

It is the Sengoku period.
Beyond peaks of deep snow lies
the land of Ashina. Sword Saint
Isshin Ashina, who led a revolution
and created this country in only
one generation, is the leader of
this northern land. Now, its very
existence is in danger.

Isshin's grandson and general of
Ashina, fearing the worst, secretly
instructs his men:

"We can no longer rely on normal
means to protect Ashina from
outsiders. We must find the Divine
Heir."

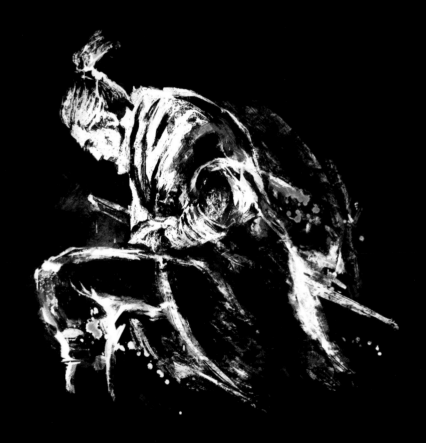

And so, the Divine Heir is captured. But he is all alone in this world, with no family or vassals—save for one shinobi.

This is the story of two lone wolves bound together by duty.

THE BLOODY ASHINA REVOLUTION

It is the end of the Sengoku period. The fires of war that burned all of Japan refuse to die, spreading even to the land of Ashina, nestled deep between tall mountains.

DEFEATED
SOLDIER

SHUZEN TAMURA VERSUS ISSHIN ASHINA

The sword saint, Isshin Ashina, in his bloody revolution.

A wolf, picked up on the battlefield.
After years of training, he emerges a master shinobi.

WOLF

THE IRON CODE

ASHINA RESERVOIR

Twenty years have passed since Isshin's revolution. Ashina is in decline, and the shinobi Wolf has lost everything.

Both his adoptive father, and the master he swore to protect…

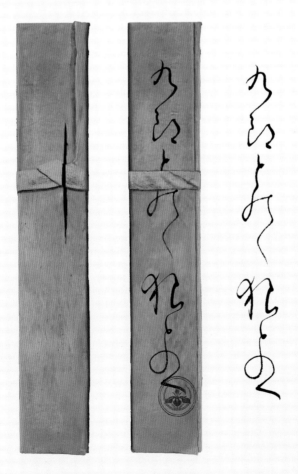

🔵 Text of the Iris

SECRET PASSAGE

MOON-VIEW
TOWER

● Moon-View Tower, Outside

Moon-View Tower
Partition Screen

DILAPIDATED
TEMPLE

TRAINING WITH
THE UNDYING

● Sculptor's Idol

SHINOBI
SECRET
PASSAGE

DILAPIDATED TEMPLE, INSIDE

🔵 Offering Box

🔵 Young Master's Bell

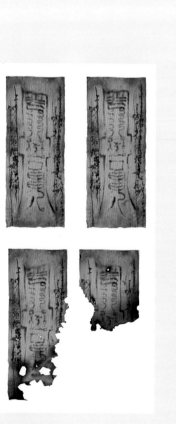

🔵 Talismans

CLIFF PATH

● Sacred Tree

LOOKOUT, ASHINA OUTSKIRTS

OUTSKIRTS WALL, INSIDE

SHADOWS DIE TWICE

SHRINE

BURIAL MOUND FOR
SEVERED HEADS

● Watchtower

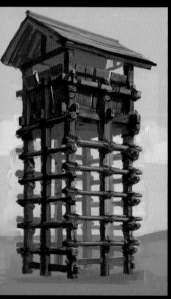

OLD
BATTLEFIELD

Blazing Bull's Courtyard

⊜ Three-Story Tower

⊜ Tower Gate

⊜ Watchtower

⊜ Bretèche

BATTLEFIELD MEMORIAL MOB

ASHINA CASTLE

CASTLE TOWER ROOF

TEA ROOM

DOCUMENTS ROOM

● Dragonspring River Folding Screen

● Audience Chamber Scroll

TOWER
WALKWAYS

● Coffered-Ceiling Images

AUDIENCE CHAMBER

🔘 Area Map

Valuables Box

Sliding-Screen Art

Upper tower—
Ashina Dojo

Ashina Dojo Folding-Screen Art

高麗橋うあやかし軍兵にあらう
その為めの玉去名もあり
吾が御妃狙怪の玉の妃を訳ひ
これに報ず

● Scroll of an Ancient Battle

Room Partition Art

CASTLE TOWER LOOKOUT

ISSHIN'S ROOM

KURO'S ROOM

● Incense Burner

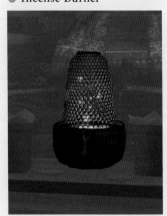

● Small Shrine

Armor

Sliding-Screen Handle

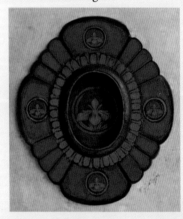

Deer Horns

CASTLE
TOWER
ENTRANCE

CASTLE
TOWER
ATRIUM

OLD GRAVE

GREAT SERPENT SHRINE, OUTSIDE

GREAT SERPENT SHRINE, INSIDE

DRAGONSPRING—HIRATA ESTATE

GRAVEKEEPER'S HOUSE

🔆 Guardhouse

GARDEN

SHADOWS DIE TWICE Official Artworks

DRAWING ROOM, INSIDE

🔵 Cave Wall

PATH TO BAMBOO-THICKET SLOPE

SERVANT'S LODGINGS

Shrine Decorated with Carp

Turtle-Shaped
Metal Fixture

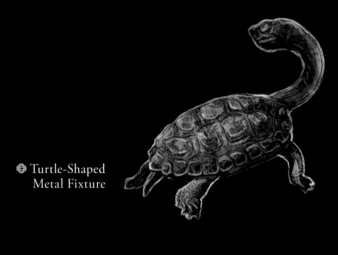

Sunshade Decoration

BAMBOO-
THICKET
SLOPE

MAIN BUILDING

MAIN BUILDING—
GARDEN ON FIRE

⊜ Bodhisattva

ABANDONED DUNGEON

DUNGEON MEMORIAL MOB

ABANDONED DUNGEON ENTRANCE

● Hook

● Makeshift Bridge

ABANDONED DUNGEON PATH

Dojun's
LABORATORY

◉ Cadaver

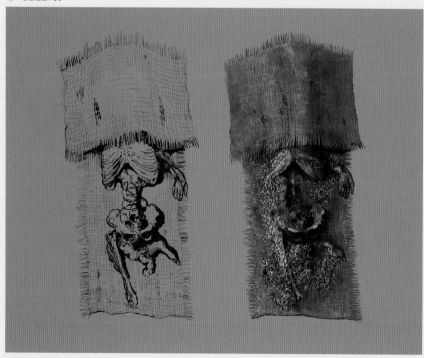

Bottomless hole

Underwater Jail

Elevator

SENPOU TEMPLE, MOUNT KONGO

TEMPLE GROUNDS

STOREHOUSE

DEVA GATE

TEMPLE GATE

⊜ Candle Stand

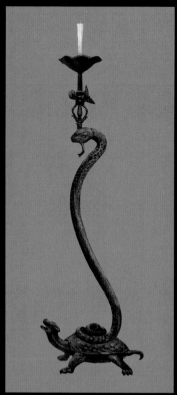

⊜ Shinobi Kite

⊜ Kite-Flying Device

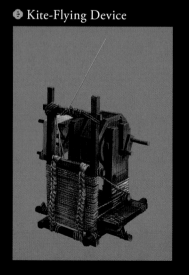

JIZO STATUES AND PINWHEELS

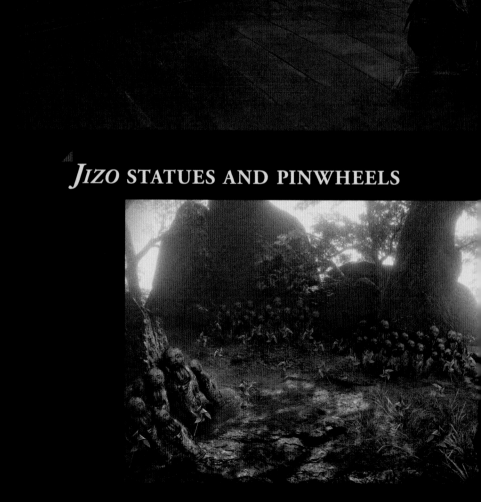

BRIDGE

POOL

FALLS

VIEW FROM THE MAIN HALL

VIEW OF THE TEMPLE

LECTURE
HALL

LECTURE
HALL,
INSIDE

MANDALA

● Bodhisattva Statue

● Decorative Metalworks

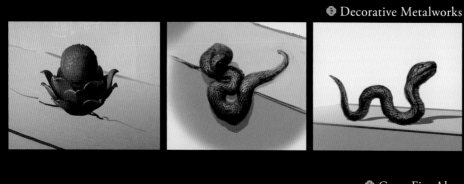

● Great Fire Altar

MAIN HALL,
INSIDE

SEKIRO: **SHADOWS DIE TWICE** Official Artworks

HALLS OF ILLUSION

112

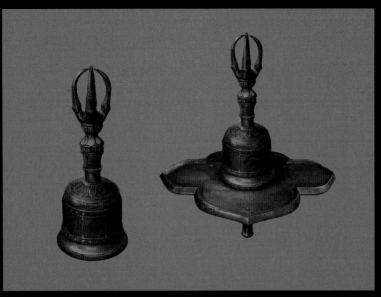

Illusive Hall Bell

ENLIGHTENED HALL

BOTTOMLESS HALL

114

ROARING HALL

MUDDY HALL

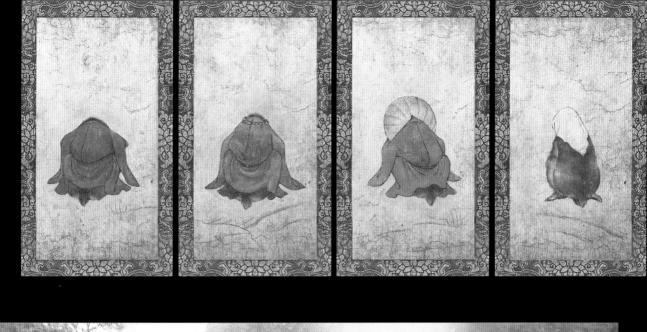

INNER SANCTUM, OUTSIDE

Folding-Screen Monkeys

INNER SANCTUM, INSIDE

SEKIRO **SHADOWS DIE TWICE** Official Artworks

● Tennyo Scrolls

FIVE-STORY TOWER, INSIDE

● Five-Story Tower

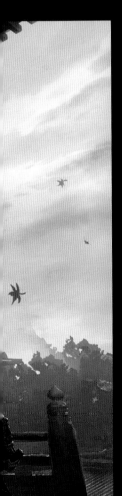

BELL DEMON'S TEMPLE

● Five-Story Tower

MAZE OF ARHAT STATUES

SEKIRO: **SHADOWS DIE TWICE** Official Artworks

GUN FORT SPIRES

◉ Snake Shrine Bodhisattva

▲ROPE
BRIDGE

GUN FORT, OUTSIDE

GUN FORT SHRINE, INSIDE

CAVERNOUS FISSURE

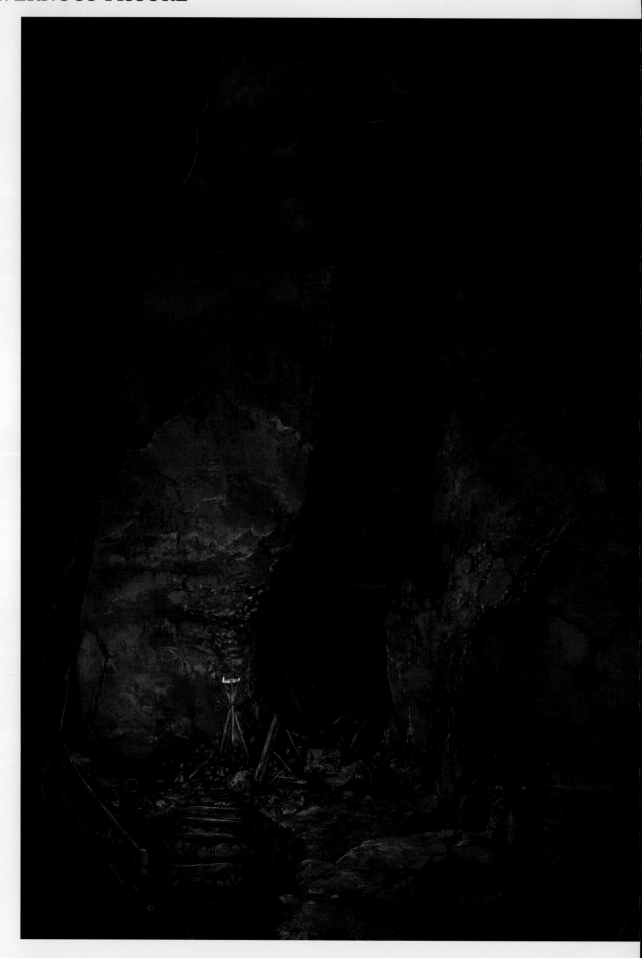

GREAT SERPENT

▲SERPENT'S NEST SHRINE

GREAT SERPENT'S NEST

● Affectionate Mother Bodhisattva Statue

BODHISATTVA VALLEY

● Sitting
Bodhisattva
Statue

● Standing
Bodhisattva
Statue

LOTUS OF THE PALACE

GUARDIAN APE'S WATERING HOLE

ASHINA DEPTHS

POISON POOL

⊜ Bodhisattva Statue

TOXIC
MEMORIAL
MOB

GUARDIAN APE'S BURROW

ABANDONED TEMPLE

Buddha of the Abandoned Temple

EXILED MEMORIAL MOB

VILLAGER HOMES, INSIDE

WEAVER HOUSE

BLOOD-SOAKED CLOTH

❸ *Gorinto*

❸ Stone Monument

❸ *Jizo* Statue

❸ Stone Lantern

RIVER BOTTOM

PRIEST'S ABODE

▲ ATTIC

▲ PRIEST'S ABODE, INSIDE

🔵 Precious
Bait

WEDDING CAVE DOOR

BURIAL STAKES

Octopus Sakura

▲SHELTER STONE

WEDDING CAVE

To the fountainhead

Vermilion bridge

Tree with Red Leaves

FOUNTAINHEAD PALACE OVERVIEW

FOUNTAINHEAD PALACE RESIDENCE, OUTSIDE

FOUNTAINHEAD PALACE RESIDENCE, INSIDE

GREAT BRIDGE TO THE PALACE GROUNDS

SHRINE

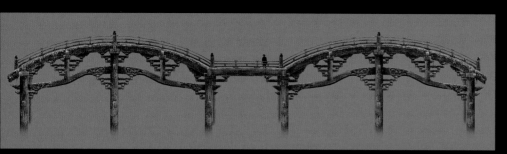

3 Great Bridge

3 Decorative Engravings

3 Decorative Roofings

3 Ox-Drawn Carriage

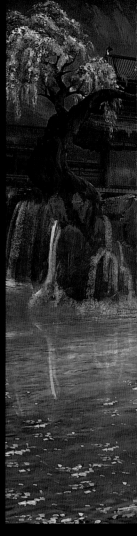

MIBU MANOR

⊜ Banner

MIBU MANOR, INSIDE

⊜ Imperial Audience Chamber

SHADOWS DIE TWICE Official Artworks

GREAT SAKURA

SEKIRO: SHADOWS DIE TWICE Official Artworks

FEEDING GROUNDS

● Summoning Bell

Underwater

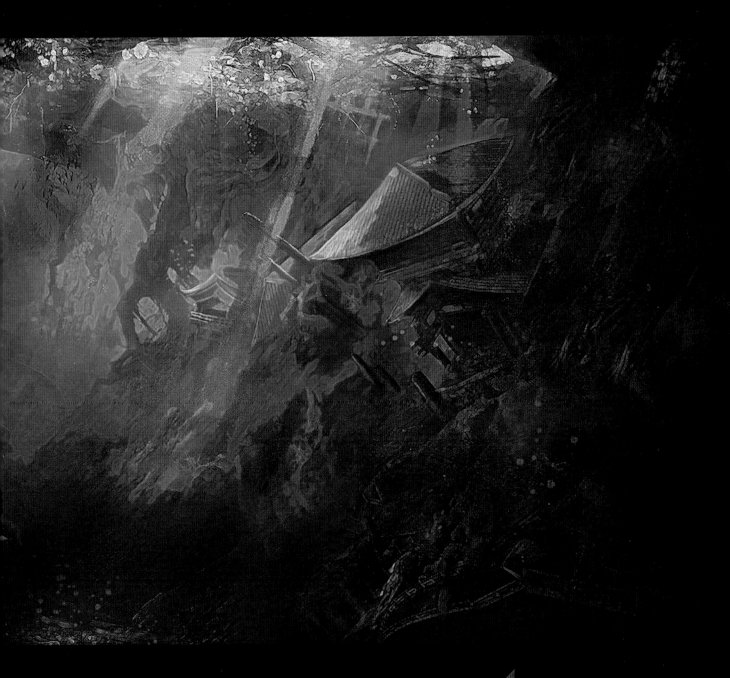

SUNKEN PALACE

Underwater cavern

Lake bed

CONSUMPTION OF THE RITUAL SACRIFICE

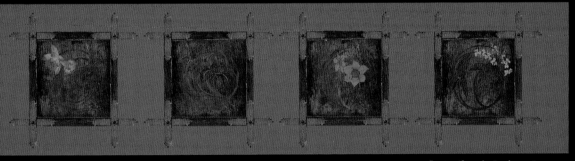

❸ Coffered-Ceiling Images

● Old Dragons of the Tree Folding Screen

● Palace Treasure Box

● Divine Dragon Folding Screen

PALACE AUDIENCE CHAMBER

PALACE
BEDROOM

SANCTUARY

STONE SHRINE

DIVINE DRAGON'S SEAT

SEKIRO: **SHADOWS DIE TWICE** Official Artworks

DIVINE REALM

INTERIOR MINISTRY'S INVASION

ASHINA CASTLE ABLAZE

INTERIOR MINISTRY ENCAMPMENT

◢Demon of Hatred

SEKIRO: **SHADOWS DIE TWICE** Official Artworks

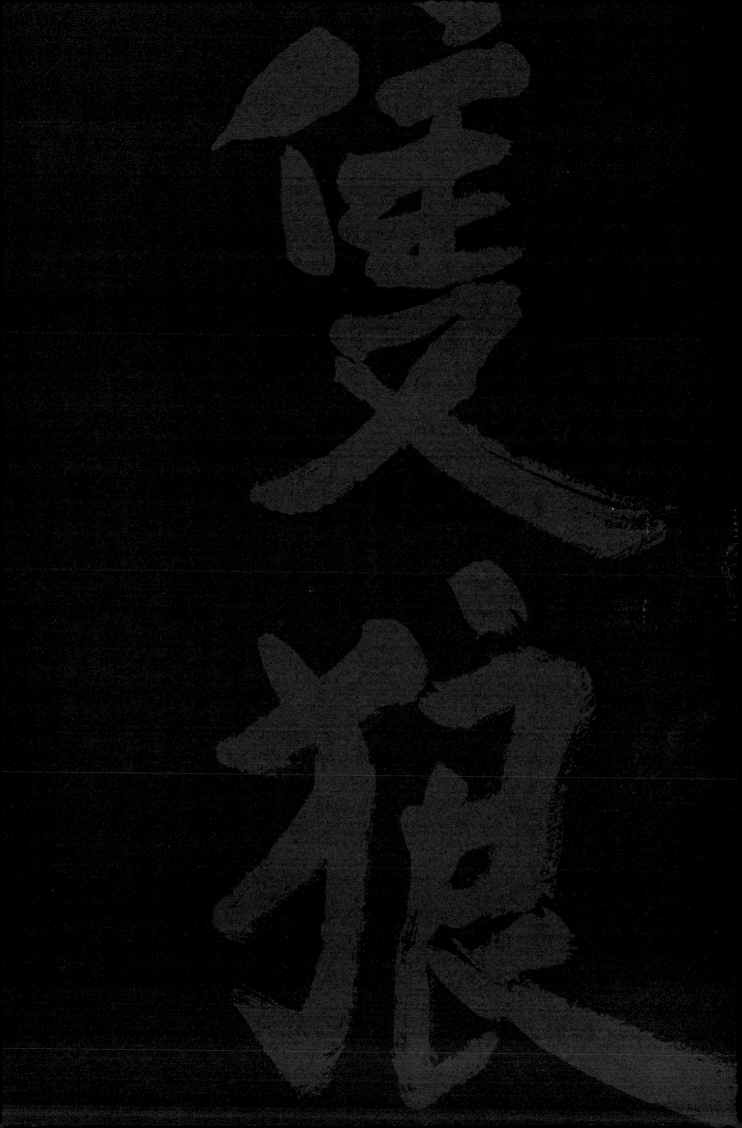

CHARACTERS
& PROSTHETIC
TOOLS

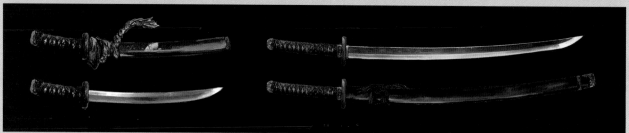

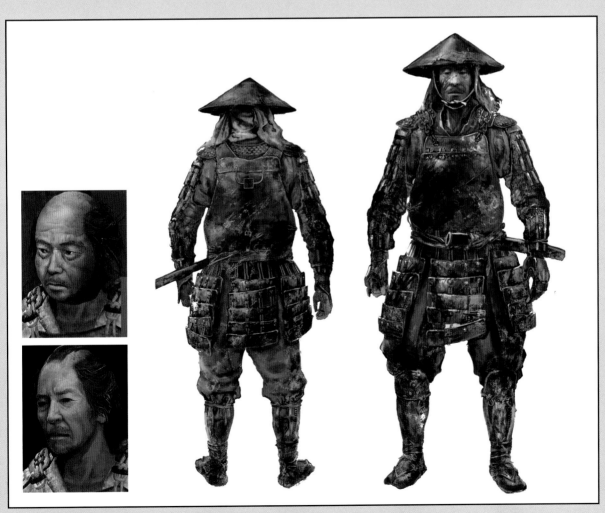

| LOW-RANKED ASHINA SOLDIER

| LOW-RANKED TAMURA SOLDIER

206

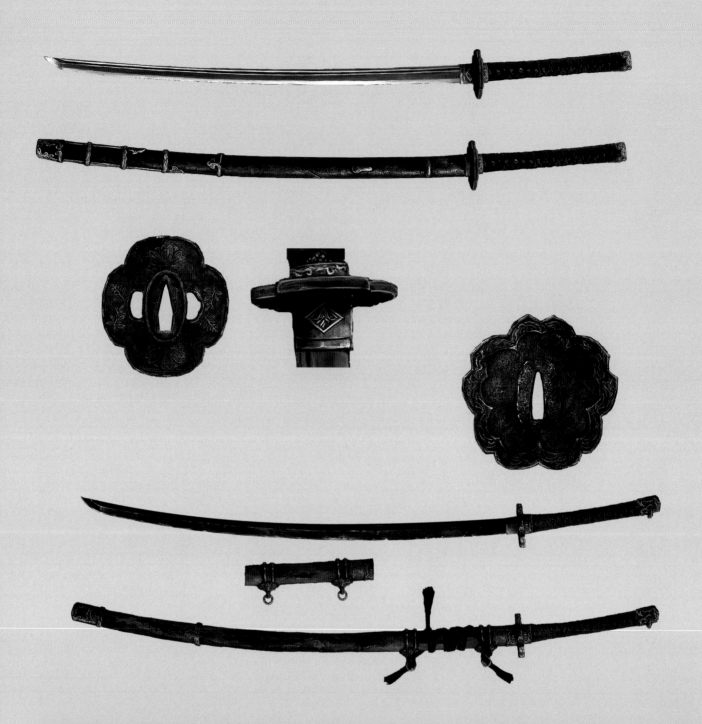

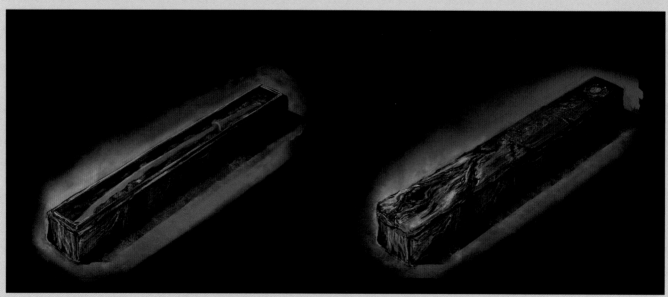

● Initial Sketch

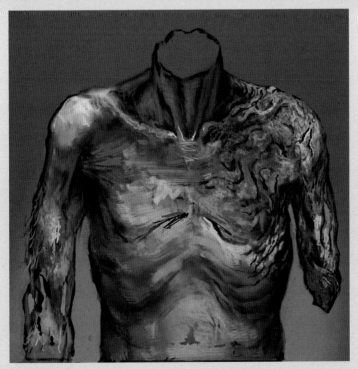

HANBEI THE UNDYING

213 SEKIRO: SHADOWS DIE TWICE Official Artworks

KURO, THE DIVINE HEIR

Initial Sketch

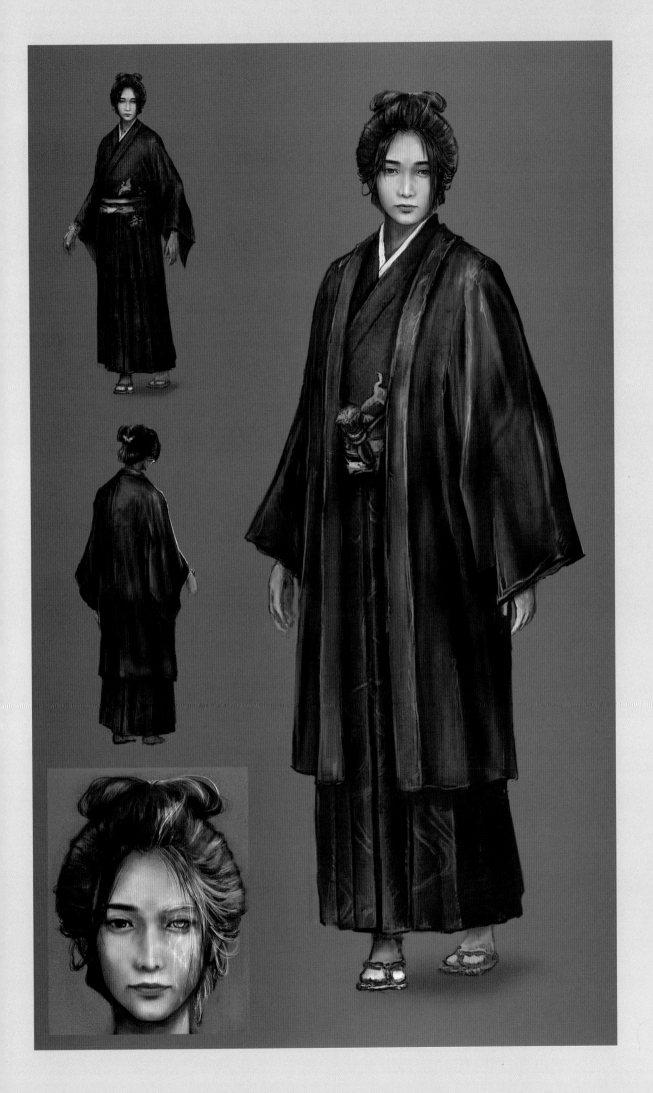

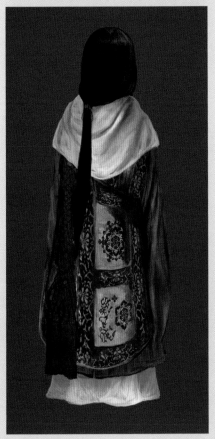

● Initial Sketch

| FAITHFUL ONE

| JINZAEMON KUMANO

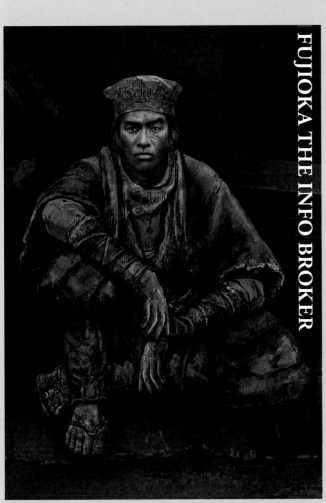

| FUJIOKA THE INFO BROKER

| MEMORIAL MOB

222

INOSUKE'S MOTHER

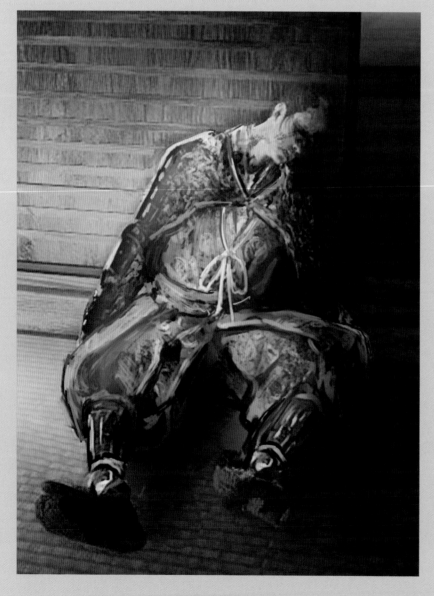

INOSUKE NOGAMI

BLACKHAT BADGER

DOJUN

MIBU PRIEST

224

ATTENDANT'S DAUGHTER
(FIRST DAUGHTER)

ATTENDANT'S DAUGHTER
(SECOND DAUGHTER)

OLD MAID

PRIESTESS

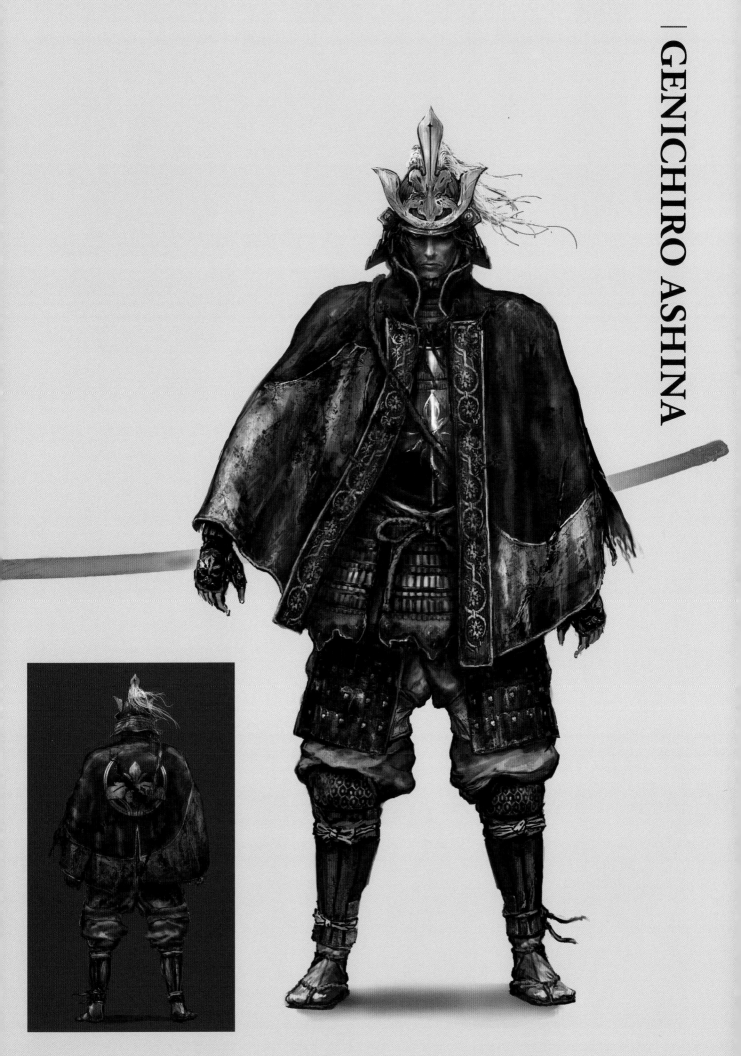

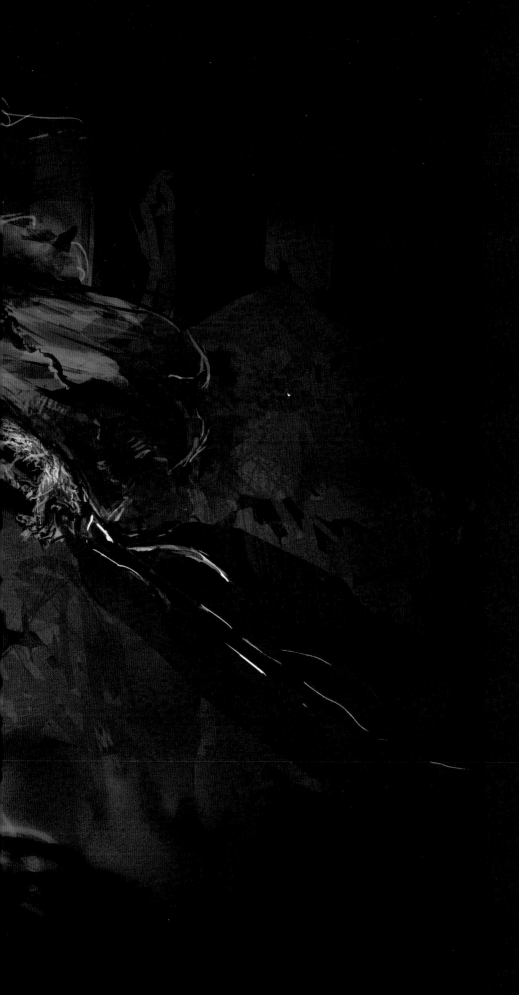

● Initial Sketch

SEKIRO: SHADOWS DIE TWICE Official Artworks

GYOUBU MASATAKA ONIWA

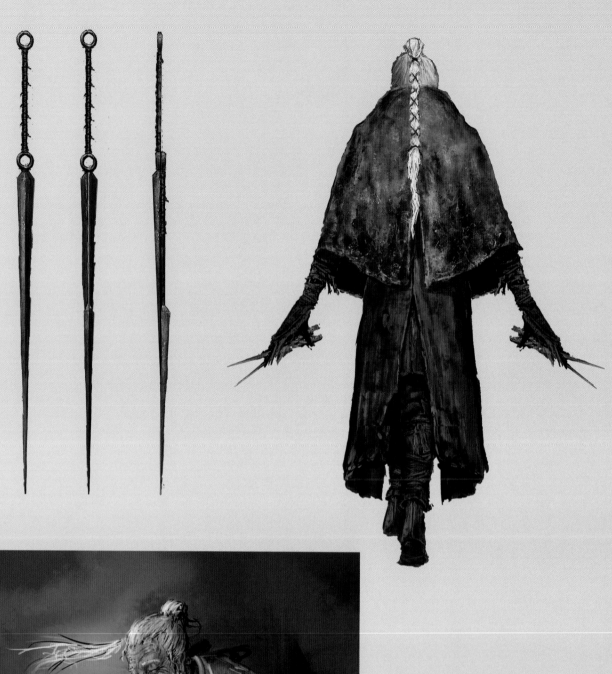

Initial Sketch

SEKIRO: SHADOWS DIE TWICE Official Artworks

GREAT COLORED CARP

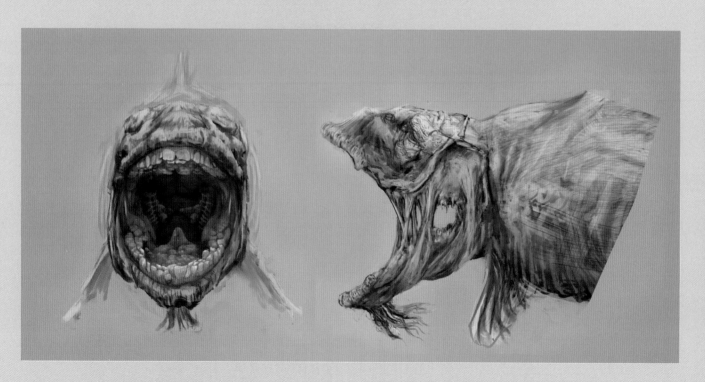

PRIESTESS YAO

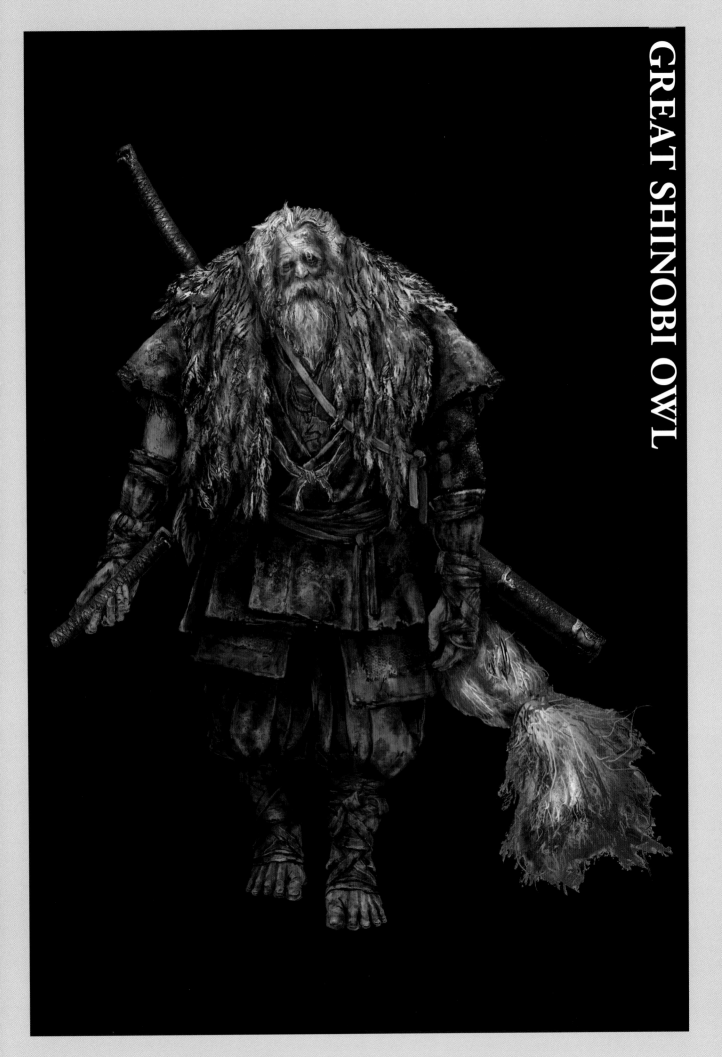

GREAT SHINOBI OWL

⑤ Initial Sketch

ISSHIN, THE SWORD SAINT

DEMON OF HATRED

SEVEN ASHINA SPEARS

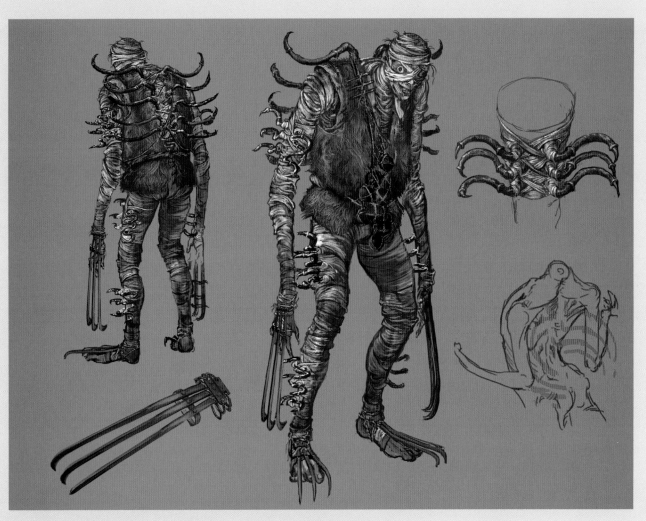

SHINOBI HUNTER

JUZOU
THE
DRUNKARD

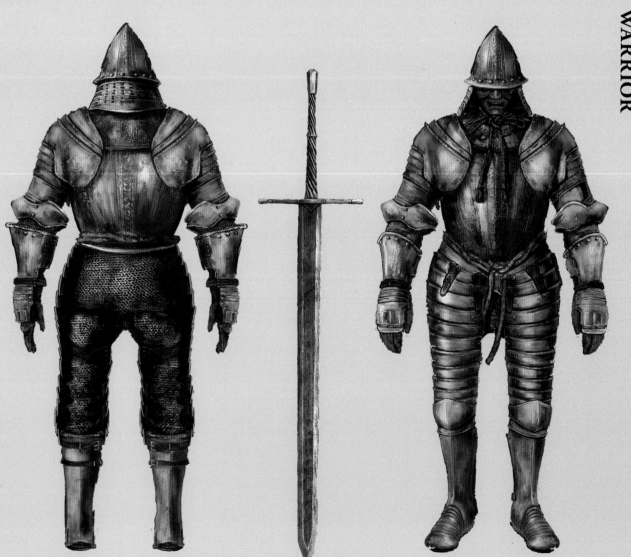

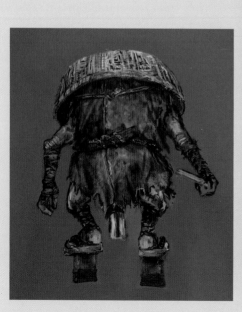

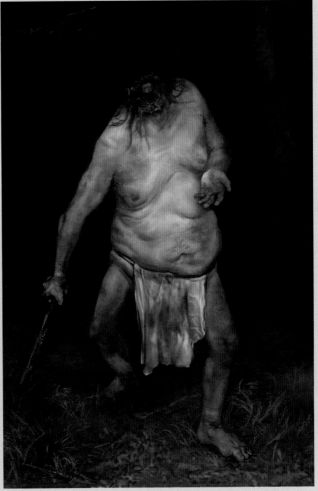

OKAMI
WARRIOR

LONE SHADOW

SHINOBI DOG

GRAVEKEEPER

BRIGAND

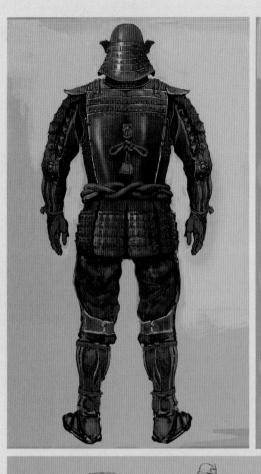

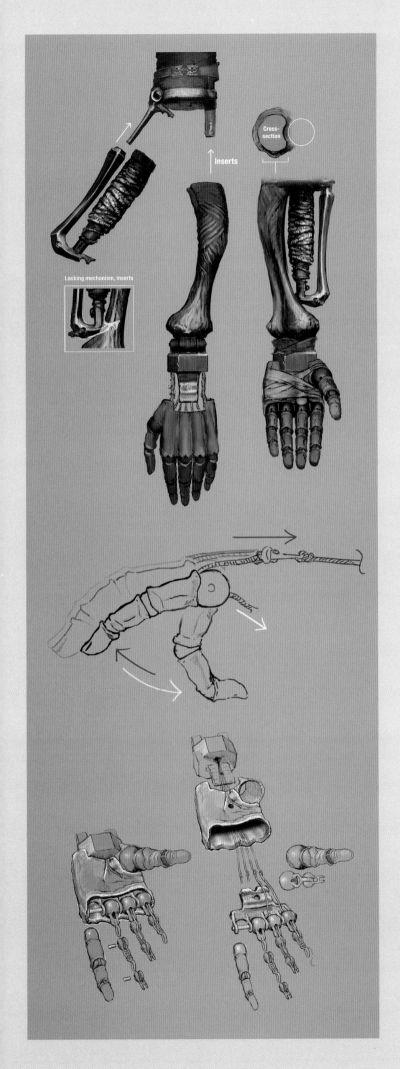

Inserts

Cross-section

Locking mechanism, inserts

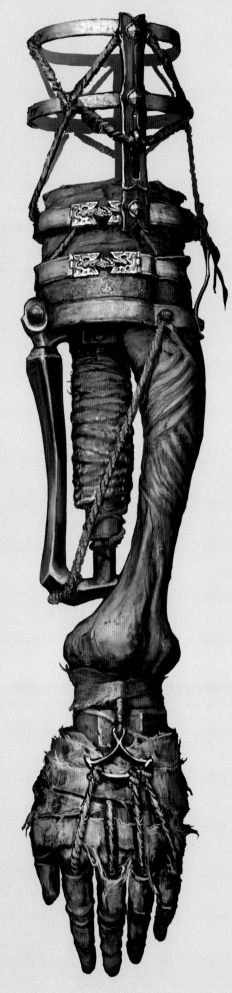

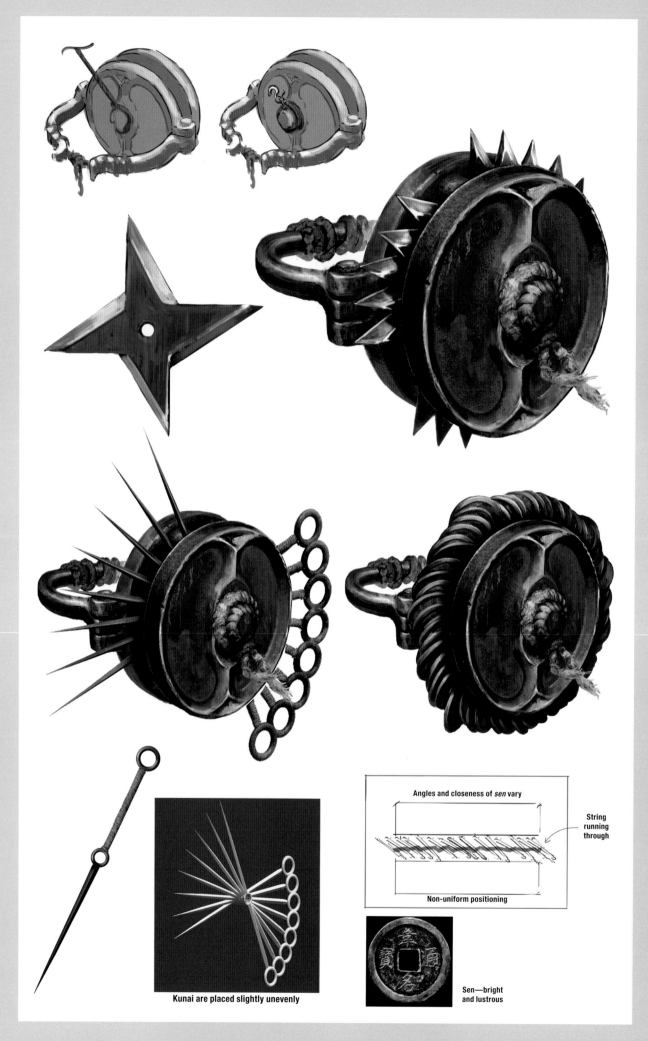

Angles and closeness of *sen* vary

String running through

Non-uniform positioning

Kunai are placed slightly unevenly

Sen—bright and lustrous

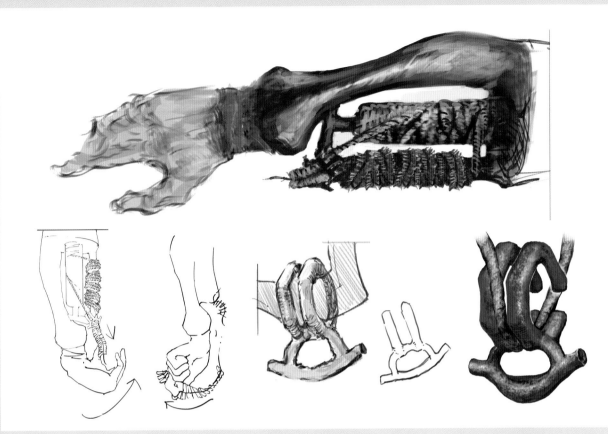

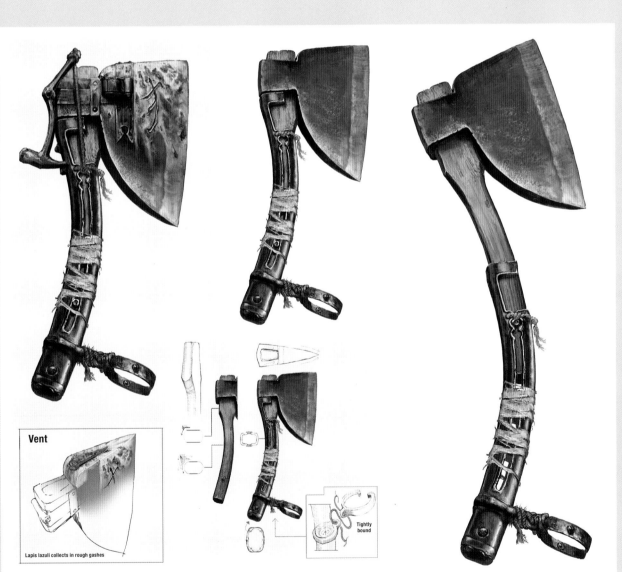

Vent

Lapis lazuli collects in rough gashes

Tightly bound

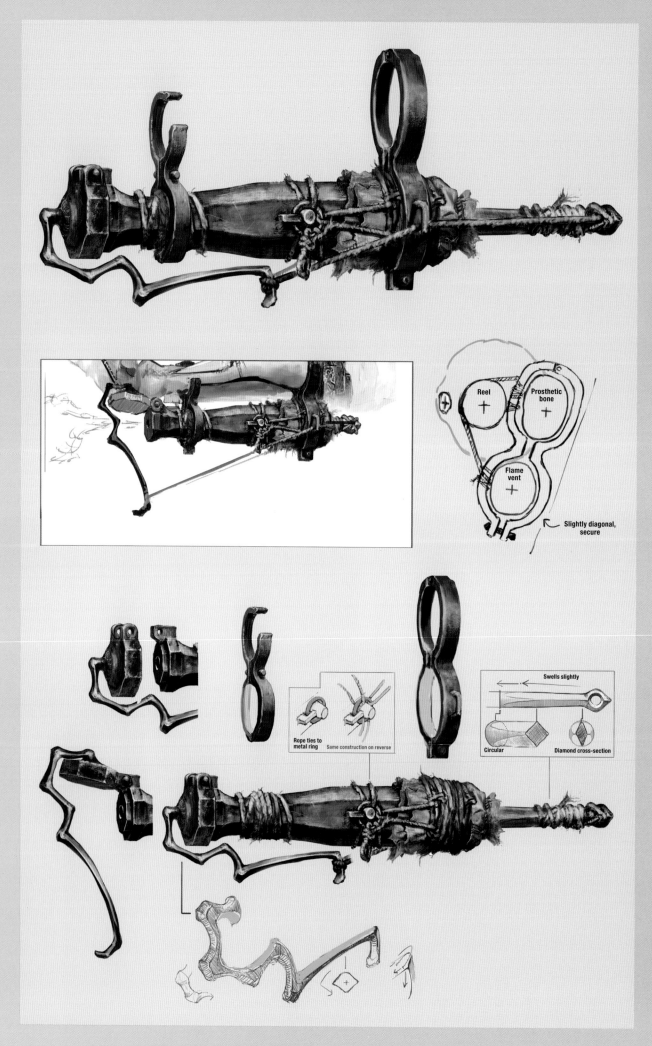

Reel

Prosthetic bone

Flame vent

Slightly diagonal, secure

Rope ties to metal ring

Same construction on reverse

Swells slightly

Circular

Diamond cross-section

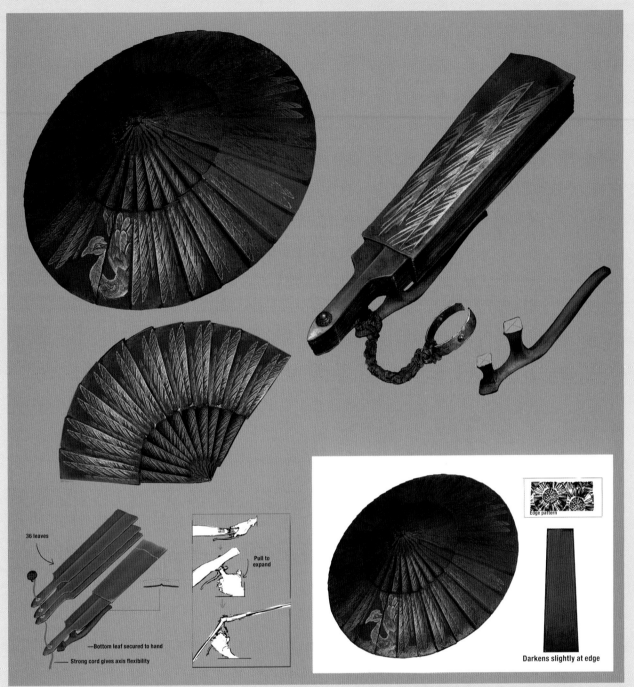

36 leaves

—Bottom leaf secured to hand

Strong cord gives axis flexibility

Pull to expand

Edge pattern

Darkens slightly at edge

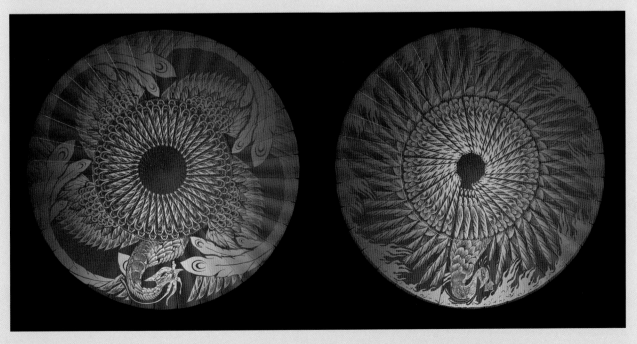

Normal

↓

Double Divine Abduction

↓

Golden Vortex

Gutters extend to inner pattern

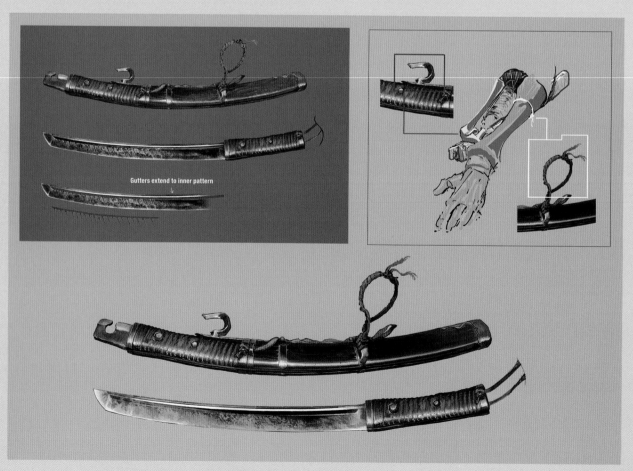

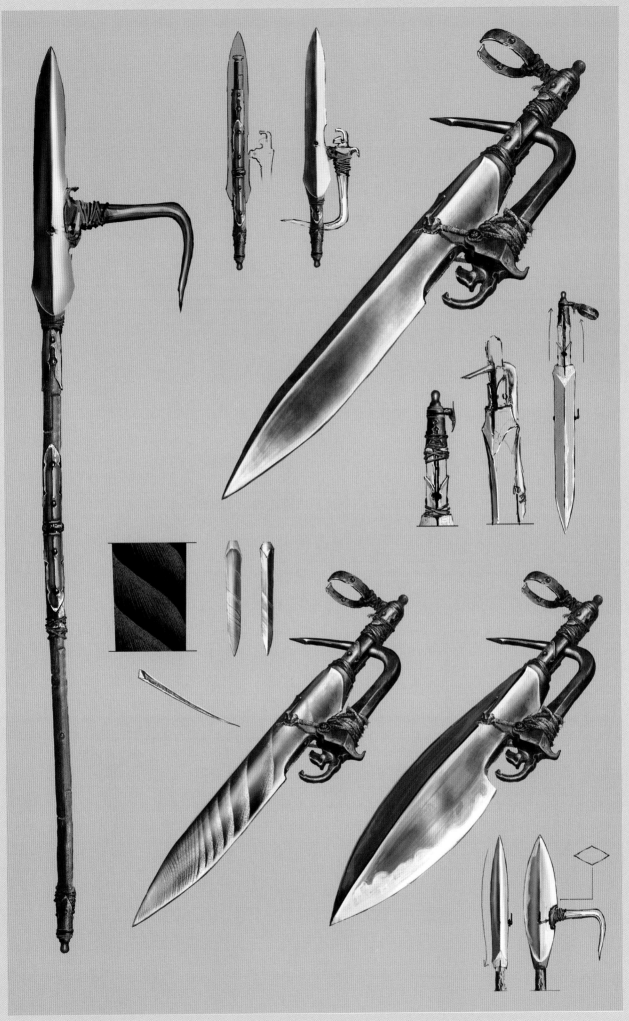

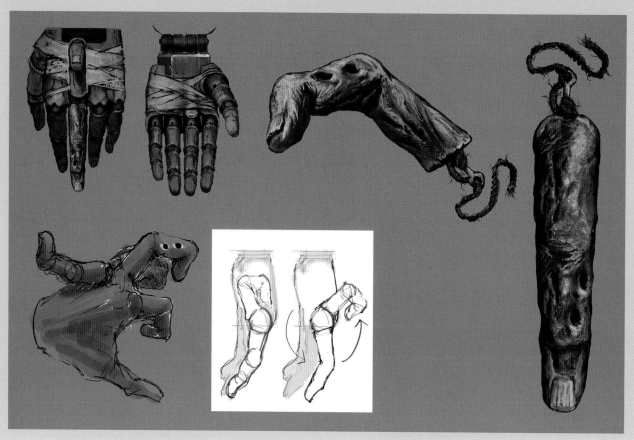

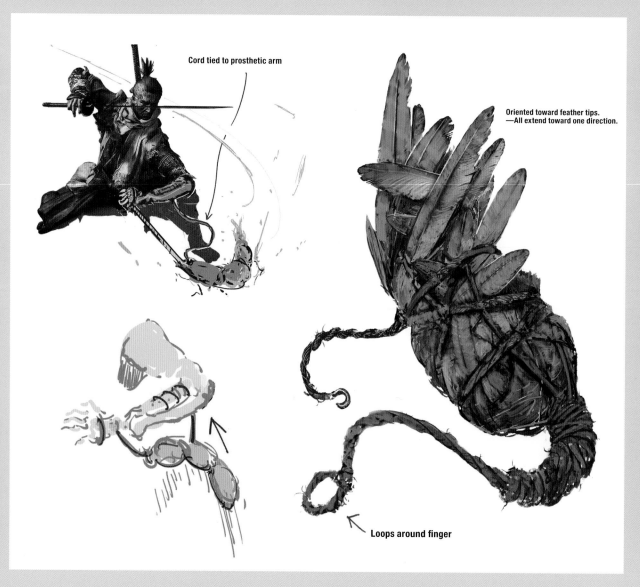

Cord tied to prosthetic arm

Oriented toward feather tips.
—All extend toward one direction.

Loops around finger

ITEMS & RELATED INFORMATION

SEKIRO
SHADOWS DIE TWICE
Official Artworks

Mechanical Barrel

A mechanical metal barrel that can be given to the Sculptor to enable Prosthetic Tool upgrades.

It appears to have been made to fit perfectly inside the wrist bone of the Shinobi Prosthetic.

A reinforced core is sure to make a shinobi's fangs even sharper.

Shinobi Prosthetic

The artificial arm of a shinobi, passed down by the Sculptor.

A replica of a human arm fitted with a variety of mechanisms, apparently designed with modification in mind.

While it bears a number of cuts and is stained thick with blood and oil, it has been impeccably maintained.

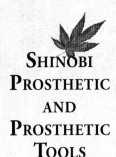

SHINOBI PROSTHETIC AND PROSTHETIC TOOLS

Mortal Blade

An *odachi* capable of slaying the undying. Its crimson blade will take the life of any who dares draw it.

Without the power of Resurrection, one could not hope to wield this weapon, which allows one to defeat even infested beings.

Long concealed within Senpou Temple, the blade is inscribed with its true name: "Gracious Gift of Tears."

Kusabimaru

A katana given by Kuro, the Divine Heir. An heirloom of the Hirata family, a cadet branch descended from Ashina.

Once thought lost, it has found its way back into the hands of the Wolf. The name Kusabimaru beseeches, "A shinobi's role is to kill, but even a shinobi must not forget mercy." A mantra the blade itself may manifest.

KATANA

***Sen* Throw**

A Prosthetic Tool that shoots loaded coin bundles. Costs *sen* and Spirit Emblems to use.

While it lacks a shuriken's range, it inflicts far more damage, as the coins hit multiple times. The amount of coins thrown increases depending on how much money one possesses. Being rich makes the blast incredibly strong, but an empty purse will shoot nothing but dust.

Phantom Kunai

Lady Butterfly's kunai, fitted into the Shuriken Wheel. Costs Spirit Emblems to use.

Creates a special sound when thrown, which causes phantom butterflies to follow the path of the kunai. The phantom butterflies chase after enemies and inflict damage even when guarded.

Gouging Top

An enhanced shuriken that pierces enemies with its sharp blades. Costs Spirit Emblems to use.

These piercing blades retain momentum after landing, and will damage an enemy's Vitality and Posture, even if guarded. Taking a moment to further bend the spring and build rotational energy will cause the blade to rotate after landing, damaging the enemy multiple times on hit.

Spinning Shuriken

An enhanced shuriken that can be empowered with rotational energy. Costs Spirit Emblems to use.

Damages an enemy's Vitality and Posture, and does huge damage to jumping enemies. Taking a moment to further bend the spring and build rotational energy will cause the blade to rotate after landing, damaging the enemy multiple times on hit.

Similar to a spinning top, but with blades.

Loaded Shuriken

A Shuriken Wheel Prosthetic Tool, fitted to the Shinobi Prosthetic. Costs Spirit Emblems to use.

Pull a shuriken loaded into the wheel and launch it at the target in a single, flowing motion. The swiftly thrown shuriken damages enemy Vitality and Posture, particularly against those with a tendency to take to the air.

Shuriken Wheel

A mechanical device made by the mechanical genius Dogen. Can be fit into the Shinobi Prosthetic to become a working Prosthetic Tool.

While it is palm-sized, a surprising number of shuriken can fit into the Shuriken Wheel, as the edges were designed for stacking.

A fine example of what can be achieved when one matches mechanical finesse with a shinobi's talent.

Purple Fume Spark

An upgraded Firecracker that uses a purple, smoke-emitting compound gunpowder. Costs Spirit Emblems to use.

The tweaked compound gunpowder is known as "Purple Fume Spark."

The addition of fatty wax lumps delays the explosion slightly.

Enemies blinded by the blast take slightly more Vitality and Posture damage for a brief period of time.

Long Spark

An upgraded Firecracker using compound gunpowder. Costs Spirit Emblems to use.

Compounded gunpowder is said to have a long spark, and by increasing the proportion of Black Gunpowder, the effect can be prolonged for longer than the average Firecracker.

The flames of the Firecrackers bloom for a short while.

Spring-Load Firecracker

A Firecracker upgraded with a spring mechanism. Costs Spirit Emblems to use.

Unleashes a loud explosion and bright flash that causes foes to recoil and inflicts Posture damage on beast-type enemies.

Charging up the spring mechanism adds rotational energy when spreading the Firecrackers, affecting enemies in all directions.

Shinobi Firecracker

A Prosthetic Tool fitted with Robert's Firecrackers. Costs Spirit Emblems.

Unleashes an explosive flash that briefly blinds foes and inflicts Posture damage on beast-type enemies. Has a wide, frontward field of effect that can impact multiple enemies at once.

Suitable for temporarily immobilizing enemies and particularly good for scaring beasts.

Robert's Firecrackers

Firecrackers from across southern seas. Can be fitted to the Shinobi Prosthetic to become a Prosthetic Tool.

Makes a deafening sound, frightening to animals. Sold by little Robert and his father to raise funds for their travels.

Their voyage brought them to Japan, where they would seek the "Undying" in an attempt to extend Robert's life.

Lazulite Shuriken

Shuriken blessed with the favor of the Fountainhead Lapis Lazuli. Costs Spirit Emblems to use.

Its piercing edge heavily damages Vitality, and damages Vitality and Posture even if guarded. These blades do not slow down, even after striking an enemy.

The lazulite-blue trail of light it emits in flight is reminiscent of a shooting star.

Shinobi Axe of the Monkey

A heavy, black, iron axe used by shinobi. Can be fitted to the Shinobi Prosthetic to become a working Prosthetic Tool.

This boorish axe is used less for cutting and more for breaking things with its weight.

Once the favored weapon of a shinobi known as the "Bounding Monkey of the Sunken Valley," it was lost along with his left arm.

Lazulite Sacred Flame

A Flame Barrel blessed with the favor of the Fountainhead Lapis Lazuli. Costs Spirit Emblems to use.

Damages even apparitions with its blazing-purple flame. The flame does not, however, inflict the "Burn" status abnormality.

The sacred lapis lazuli fires are divine. Cleanse the deep-seated hatred with flame.

Okinaga's Flame Vent

A barrel containing smoldering resin that acts as an explosive catalyst. Costs Spirit Emblems to use.

Emits a short-range flame blast. Continuous fire damage will inflict the "Burn" status.

It is able to maintain a continuous stream of flames due to the smoldering resin inside the tube mechanism.

Spring-Load Flame Vent

A Flame Barrel fitted with a gunpowder-loaded mechanism. Costs Spirit Emblems to use.

Deals damage to enemies with gouts of fire, inflicting the "Burn" status abnormality. The spring mechanism can also be charged to release a massive blast of flames and hot air, sending opponents flying.

Flame Vent

A Prosthetic Tool made from a loaded Flame Barrel. Costs Spirit Emblems to use.

Deals fire damage to enemies via a short-range blast of fire while also inflicting the "Burn" status.

It is difficult to control the rage of those with red eyes through the power of man alone. They do, however, fear the flame above all else. This tool has the power to make them tremble.

Flame Barrel

An iron barrel that spews fire. Can be fitted to the Shinobi Prosthetic to become a Prosthetic Tool.

It is difficult to control the rage-filled Red-eyes with the power of man alone.

However, a fire-based weapon could be a means of resisting them. They are said to fear fire above all else.

Sabimaru

A Prosthetic Tool made with the blade Sabimaru, allowing for a quick series of attacks together with the sword.

The blue, poisonous rust on Sabimaru's blade applies the "Poison" status abnormality. Wielded in wars of old, the blade's blue rust was used to drive off inhuman Okami warrior women. Even now, it is likely to be effective against their descendants.

Sabimaru

An ancient *kodachi* short sword, its blade mottled with bluish rust. Can be fitted to the Shinobi Prosthetic to create a Prosthetic Tool.

Forged by the Ashina clan to resist the inhuman evil that had invaded Ashina in times long forgotten. It was the poisonous gift of the blue rust that finally drove the spirits out.

Lazulite Axe

A Loaded Axe blessed with the favor of the Fountainhead Lapis Lazuli. Costs Spirit Emblems to use.

The hefty lazulite blade inflicts damage even on guarding enemies. The sound of the lapis-lazuli blade striking home creates a powerful reverberation capable of dispelling enemy illusions.

Sparking Axe

A Loaded Axe with an attached percussion hammer to create flame. Costs Spirit Emblems to use.

Metes out attacks bathed in flame from the axe's blade. Hitting the sparking percussion hammer causes a violent eruption of flames and increases the effective area of the attack.

This is both a firearm and a heavy axe.

Spring-Load Axe

A Loaded Axe reinforced with a spring mechanism. Costs Spirit Emblems to use.

The strength of the Loaded Axe lies in its heft. The weight allows one to shrug off incoming attacks and can easily turn a wooden shield into splinters.

Storing and unleashing energy in the spring mechanism allows for large, sweeping attacks despite its weight.

Loaded Axe

A Prosthetic Tool loaded with a heavy Shinobi Axe. Costs Spirit Emblems to use.

The strength of the Loaded Axe lies in its heft.

One strike can easily turn a wooden shield into splinters or shred an enemy's Posture.

Loaded Spear Thrust Type

A Loaded Spear reinforced with a spring mechanism. Costs Spirit Emblems to use.

Allows for long-range thrust attacks. Lighter enemies struck by the attacks may be dragged toward the wielder. Can also tear poorly fitting armor from heavier foes.

Store energy in the spring mechanism and use its momentum for successive and relentless thrust attacks.

Loaded Spear

A Prosthetic Tool loaded with Gyoubu's Broken Horn. Costs Spirit Emblems to use.

Unleash far-reaching thrust attacks. Lighter enemies struck by the spear may be dragged toward the wielder.

Those of large build will at times force themselves into poorly fitting armor. Such armor could be torn clean off—coined by Gyoubu as Armor Stripping.

Gyoubu's Broken Horn

Famed horn-spear once used by Gyoubu Masataka Oniwa. Affix to the Shinobi Prosthetic to create a Prosthetic Tool.

The horn contracts to pull enemies in, and is also capable of stripping crude armor. When the horn was broken during the rebellion, Isshin praised it for its "splendid shape," awarding Oniwa with the cross-bladed spear of Shuzen Tamura.

Lazulite Sabimaru

Sabimaru blessed with the favor of the Fountainhead Lapis Lazuli. Costs Spirit Emblems to use.

The combination of the Lapis Lazuli and the rusted blue blade produces a poisonous mist with every swing.

Dissolving the Lapis Lazuli over the blade caused the ancient blue rust to bubble to the blade's surface.

Piercing Sabimaru

A further improved Sabimaru with a finely sharpened blade. Costs Spirit Emblems to use.

Repeated attacks with the newly sharpened edge of the blade will damage an enemy's Vitality and Posture, even through their guard.

The blue-rust poison on Sabimaru's blade eats its way into enemies and applies the "Poison" status.

Improved Sabimaru

An improved Sabimaru with a special mechanism for unleashing the blade. Costs Spirit Emblems to use.

Due to the revised mechanism, one can fluidly swap between two separate sets of attacks as desired.

Has a blue-rust poison applied to the blade that eats into enemies' defense and inflicts the "Poison" status abnormality.

Loaded Umbrella - Magnet

A Loaded Umbrella upgraded with a magnetic mechanism. Costs Spirit Emblems to use.

When spread open, it will protect against attacks from all directions. Hold it out while moving to protect from light attacks. Has a tempered magnetic shaft that makes it nearly unbreakable. Enemy attacks can be deflected by spinning the open umbrella.

Loaded Umbrella

A Prosthetic Tool created by fitting an indestructible iron-ribbed umbrella to the Arm. Costs Spirit Emblems to use.

When spread open, it will protect against attacks from all directions. Hold it out while moving to protect from light attacks.

But this is an umbrella, after all—it won't protect you from low attacks such as sweep attacks.

Iron Fortress

An iron fan made in the far west.

Can be fitted into the Shinobi Prosthetic to become a working Prosthetic Tool.

Experienced iron-ribbed fan users can deflect arrows and even bullets using this tool.

Passed down through generations of assassins serving Senpou Temple, it wouldn't be surprising if the next owner decided its weight was impractical.

Leaping Flame

A Loaded Spear with an attached percussion hammer to create flame. Costs Spirit Emblems to use.

Bathe the tip of the Loaded Spear in flames, making it a dangerously sharp spear and firearm.

A charged strike of the spear will knock enemies down and consume them in a fiery blaze.

Spiral Spear

A Loaded Spear with a spiral chiseled into the blade. Costs Spirit Emblems to use.

Sharp thrust attacks from this Prosthetic Tool damage an enemy's Vitality and Posture, even through their guard.

The spear's spiral creates a corkscrew shockwave that gouges and rends as it penetrates.

Loaded Spear Cleave Type

A Loaded Spear further reinforced with an enhanced spring mechanism. Costs Spirit Emblems to use.

Unleash far-reaching thrust attacks. Lighter enemies struck by the spear may be dragged towards the wielder. Can also tear poorly fitting armor from heavier foes.

Store energy in the spring mechanism for a powerful cleaving attack.

Golden Vortex

A large and withered golden fan. Costs Spirit Emblems to use.

Gather illustrious golden wind and release it to force enemies caught up in the vortex to face the other way. Can be performed twice in a row.

Enemies that have been turned around drop items or money, to be considered "donations."

Double Divine Abduction

A large fan that creates a vortex of wind. Costs Spirit Emblems to use. Gathers and releases a gust of wind, forcing enemies caught by the blast to turn around. Can be waved twice in succession.

It is a mild sort of being spirited away that can be returned from quite quickly.

However, it's said that one can only return from being spirited away once, and if taken again, there is no coming back.

Divine Abduction

A Prosthetic Tool loaded with a large fan. Costs Spirit Emblems to use. Gathers and releases a gust of wind, forcing enemies caught by the vortex to turn around.

It is a mild sort of being spirited away that can be returned from quite quickly. However, it's said that one can only return from being spirited away once, and if taken again, there is no coming back.

Large Fan

A large fan made of dyed red Japanese aralia leaves. Can be fit to the Shinobi Prosthetic to become a Prosthetic Tool.

Fanning it creates a large vortex of wind, spiriting away those it catches.

"Divine Abduction through an eight-handed fan. Once is fine, but twice and you'll never return. If abducted, we'll head to Mt. Kongo. At Senpou Temple, we'll perform virtuous deeds."

Suzaku's Lotus Umbrella

A Loaded Umbrella emblazoned with a bright-red, vermilion bird. Costs Spirit Emblems to use.

When spread open, it will protect against attacks from all directions. Hold it out while moving to protect from light attacks.

The blessing of the vermilion bird prevents damage from fire-based attacks and also prevents buildup of the "Burn" status.

Phoenix's Lilac Umbrella

A Loaded Umbrella emblazoned with a purplish-blue phoenix. Costs Spirit Emblems to use.

When spread open, it will protect against attacks from all directions. Hold it out while moving to protect from light attacks.

The blessings of the phoenix fill the umbrella, preventing damage from apparition-type enemies.

Slender Finger
The slender finger of a young woman. Can be fitted to the Shinobi Prosthetic to create a Prosthetic Tool.

Found in the belly of the Guardian Ape, it is partially digested. There is a shinobi technique called the Finger Whistle that can drive beasts wild.

The one who used it before clearly used it for this purpose, as evidenced by the finger's open hole.

Great Feather Mist Raven
Mist Raven fused with crimson feathers. Costs Spirit Emblems to use.

Disappear and displace, like the mist. Can be performed from both the assumed stance and after taking damage. Dyed red to resemble the Great Mist Raven.

The feathers vanish in a scorching wake. The great raven is a god of the land, and the touch of gods is to be feared.

Aged Feather Mist Raven
Mist Raven feathers with notches in the tips. Costs Spirit Emblems to use.

Disappear like the mist and move away. Can be performed not only from the assumed stance, but also after taking damage.

The slight notches in the tips of the feathers give the appearance of an old Mist Raven. They are there to allow one to dissolve into the mist even more easily.

Mist Raven
A Prosthetic Tool loaded with the feather of a Mist Raven. Costs Spirit Emblems to use.

When attacked in the assumed stance, disappear like the mist and move away.

Once you think you've caught one, all that will remain is feathers. That is the mark of a true Mist Raven.

Mist Raven's Feathers
A bundle of Mist Raven feathers. Can be fitted to the Shinobi Prosthetic to create a Prosthetic Tool. In Usui Forest, far to the north of Ashina, live many mysterious birds of prey.

The Mist Raven is the only one to have eluded capture by all who have tried. Should you somehow manage it, you'll find it gone, with only feathers in your grasp.

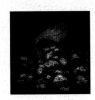

Scrap Magnetite
Magnetic ore mined in Ashina.

Base material commonly used in Prosthetic Tool upgrades of intermediate and higher rank.

Forging with magnetite produces a hard steel—a precious commodity in Ashina. Bedrock offering up this ore is constantly mined out, making it a rare one at that.

Scrap Iron
Iron dregs mined in Ashina. Widely used for basic reinforcement, it can serve as a base material for Prosthetic Tool upgrades.

Ashina is burdened with thick snow and infertile land, but the scrap iron dug from her soil is anything but crude.

UPGRADE MATERIALS

Malcontent
Finger Whistle reinforced with the Malcontent's ring. Costs Spirit Emblems to use. Can be used to drive beasts mad and to torment apparition-type enemies.

"Kingfisher" is etched onto the ring. The Kingfisher's cry could be heard along the waterfront of Sunken Valley. Now, she cries no more.

Mountain Echo
A Finger Whistle that can create an echo effect. Costs Spirit Emblems to use.

Its sound will grab an enemy's attention and draw them to the whistle's location. By locking on to a target, only the targeted enemy will hear the whistle.

Taking a deep breath before performing a whistle allows for the sound to be delayed.

Finger Whistle
A Prosthetic Tool created by fitting a slender finger to the prosthetic. Costs Spirit Emblems to use.

Its sound will grab an enemy's attention and draw them to the whistle's location. By locking on to a target, only the targeted enemy will hear the whistle.

The sound of the Finger Whistle enrages beasts, making them unable to distinguish friend from foe.

Lump of Grave Wax
A lump of fatty wax that has formed inside the body and turned pitch-black.

Used for occultic Prosthetic Tool upgrades of an advanced nature.

A long-suffered illness will see the growth turn large and blacker still. It is customary to run water over the site of an extracted growth.

Lump of Fat Wax
These lumps of fatty wax form inside the body in rare circumstances.

Can be used for intermediate and higher occultic upgrades for Prosthetic Tools.

Considered omens of disease, they are known to grow larger as the illness worsens. It's best not to let one grow any larger after it turns brown.

Fulminated Mercury
Highly precious grains forming the base for a devastating form of gunpowder.

Used in explosive Prosthetic Tool upgrades of advanced rank.

Created in secret by the Interior Ministry using knowledge from across southern seas: The central forces' military might owes much to this tiny tweak of chemistry.

Yellow Gunpowder
Amber-colored grains forming the base for powerful gunpowder. A precious commodity only found in the Sunken Valley.

Used for explosive Prosthetic Tool upgrades of intermediate and higher rank.

The yield from yellow powder is greater than that of black, lending the valley stronghold defenses their fiery vigor.

Black Gunpowder
Black grains forming the base for gunpowder.

Material used in alchemical Prosthetic Tool upgrades, including those of an explosive and occultic nature.

Even the most mundane form of gunpowder has a wide variety of applications.

Adamantite Scrap
Adamantite ore with a dull, silvery shine.

Base material commonly used in advanced Prosthetic Tool upgrades.

Adamantite can only be mined in the oldest parts of Ashina. Ancient rock and soil is said to attract the grace of gods, perhaps lending this metal its supple strength.

Pine Resin Ember
A piece of resin that contains a continuously smoldering flame. Can be used to upgrade the Flame Vent.

The resin was found in a black pine within the forests of Mibu Village. The ever-smoldering flames acted as a landmark to find one's way to the village. In time, the villagers came to loathe the flames, and the black pines were lost. Those who defended the flame were equally loathed.

Malcontent's Ring
An old ring well suited for slender fingers. "Kingfisher" is engraved on the underside. Can be used to upgrade the Finger Whistle Prosthetic Tool.

Wearing this ring as you blow the Finger Whistle will create a somber tune. The weeping voice is full of solitude and beauty. Possibly somber enough to temporarily quell a voice of rage.

Phantom Kunai
A kunai used by Lady Butterfly that can be used to upgrade the Loaded Shuriken.

A ringing sound is heard when the kunai is thrown, and phantom butterflies appear in the kunai's trail.

Since childhood, Lady Butterfly had accumulated much experience in Usui's forest, far from civilization along Tozan Trail. His forest is filled with mist and mystifications, making it ideal for training in illusion techniques.

Lapis Lazuli
Precious azure lazulite, used for the highest level of Prosthetic Tool upgrades.

Fountainhead lazulite is a symbol of eternity, and anything forged with it will never break nor rust thanks to the blessing of the Divine Dragon. Tools forged with lazulite transcend human intellect and are dubbed treasures of the Divine Dragon.

UPGRADE ITEMS

Prayer Bead
A loose prayer bead. Offering four of them at a Sculptor's Idol will increase maximum Vitality and Posture.

First Prayer Necklace
The ferocity of Ashina's army is renowned throughout the nation. Its generals are especially talented, every one of them accomplished in the Ashina sword style.

Second Prayer Necklace
In Ashina, there is a towering, pink ogre of a man, said to have gone red-eyed and run amok before he was long shut away in a forsaken dungeon...

Third Prayer Necklace
The bull was a fiery, rampaging beast and nothing more. In the last great war, the corpses of Ashina samurai piled high. Something had to be done.

Fourth Prayer Necklace
Only those who have mastered the Ashina blade may set foot inside the castle dojo. Isshin will often stop by unannounced, just to keep the students on their toes.

Fifth Prayer Necklace
The gun fort of the Sunken Valley is commanded by the Snake Eyes, an elite force of women able to pierce distant targets with mighty flint cannons and phenomenal vision.

Sixth Prayer Necklace
The Centipedes will seek out a leader, often changing names out of loyalty. Centipede chiefs are known as "Long-Arms" for their large, talon-like weapons.

Seventh Prayer Necklace
An unrivaled sumo wrestler once served a great feudal lord. Dismissed after giving up drink, he fell to a life of brigandry. And so he was dubbed Juzou the Drunkard.

Eighth Prayer Necklace
Lone Shadows are the Interior Ministry's most trusted agents. Each of leader Masasuna Oribe's sevenceenborn has a specialty, from poison to shinobi hounds.

Ninth Prayer Necklace
Robert's father came from afar across seas to the south, in search of the Undying. Repelling a thousand blades was a small price for the blessing of rejuvenation...

Final Prayer Necklace
The Seven Spears of Ashina were pivotal in Isshin's coup. He awarded the lance to none but his most loyal samurai. Yet now, only a few of the Seven remain.

Dancing Dragon Mask
A dragon's head dancing mask, made whole by piecing the fragments back together. Grants the ability to exchange Skill Points for Attack Power in the Sculptor's Idol menu.
The Okami warrior women would wear this to the Fountainhead Palace. There, they would dance as an offering for the dragon. Mysteriously, the ritual left them brimming with vigor.

Mask Fragment: Dragon
A fragment of an old dancer's mask. The original must have been broken into several pieces, and this fragment appears to be the decoration at the top of the mask.

Mask Fragment: Right
A fragment of an old dancer's mask. The original must have been broken into several pieces, and this fragment appears to be the right side of the mask.

Mask Fragment: Left
A fragment of an old dancer's mask. The original must have been broken into several pieces, and this fragment appears to be the left side of the mask.

Sakura Droplet
Pale-pink crystal residue known to form when an immortal oath fails to establish.
Increases Resurrective Power to allow an additional resurrection.
To repeat the vows of the undying and be awarded Resurrective Power once more surely necessitates the aid of a Divine Child of the Dragon's Heritage.

Gourd Seed
Seed from which healing waters continuously spring forth. Give to Emma to increase the maximum uses of the Healing Gourd.
The twisted gourd of medicinal waters was known throughout Ashina since long ago, but it was the extraordinary healer Dogen and his pupil Emma who discovered the self-replenishing nature of this seed.

USABLE ITEMS

Ceremonial Tanto
Dagger with a stark, white blade and hilt. Converts Vitality into Spirit Emblems.
Originally, this tanto was used in a ritual offering to the dragon, in which an emblem would be cut from one's own life force and set adrift on the Fountainhead waters. The blade is inscribed with its true name: "Devoted Soul."

Illusive Hall Bell
A five-pronged bell made of aged bronze. Can be used repeatedly.
When rung, Monkeys and Wolves alike are returned to their initial states. However, a Monkey caught in the folding screen will not escape, whether the bell is rung or not.

Nightjar Monocular
A bamboo tube used to see distant objects.
While shinobi already have good vision, looking through this tube with one eye enables one to see even farther.
The Nightjar Ninja serve Isshin Ashina, guarding the rooftops of Ashina Castle, their sharp eyes on the lookout for any would-be trespassers. Not much escapes the eyes of a Nightjar.

Homeward Idol
A small, palm-sized, wooden Buddha. Can be used repeatedly. Held by the Wolf ever since he was saved by his father, its corners are rounded with use. This Buddha is used to return home. It will return the user to the last visited Sculptor's Idol or the Dilapidated Temple.

Pellet
Medicinal pellets that slowly restore Vitality. A secret treatment passed down for generations in these lands, records say it has been used in battles since times long gone and lent to the famed resilience of Ashina warriors. A pill case full of these pellets would also serve as a battle charm.

Five-Color Rice
A gourd with five-colored rice used by shinobi as landmarks.
Intended to be spread on the ground in recognizable patterns. The white gourd is blessed with fertility, and resting at a Sculptor's Idol will replenish it. This rice is not edible, however.

Mottled Purple Gourd
A curved, mottled purple gourd filled with medicinal water. Refills upon rest. Reduces "Terror" status buildup and increases Terror resistance.
This gourd's twisted form was formed in graveyards, corpse-strewn battlefields, and other forlorn places of death. It follows then that drinking its waters can help prevent the onset of Terror.

Withered Red Gourd
A curved, withered red gourd filled with medicinal water. The gourd's medicine refills upon rest.
Reduces Burn buildup and lightly increases Burn resistance. It cannot heal the "Burn" status abnormality, however.

Green Mossy Gourd
A curved, moss-covered gourd filled with medicinal water. Refills upon rest. While it does not heal the "Poison" status, it reduces Poison buildup and increases Poison resistance.
This gourd was made out of necessity by those who made poisonous lands their home. It's said if you live there long enough, eventually, poison won't affect you at all.

Healing Gourd
A gourd filled with Vitality-restoring medicine. Resting refills the Gourd. Made by an apprentice of the extraordinary doctor Dogen. Though it is strange that the gourd's medicinal waters refill automatically, the seeds within may hold the secret to how it works.

Taro Persimmon

A conspicuously red persimmon at the peak of its ripeness, commonly called a "Taro persimmon."

Greatly increases Posture recovery for a time, even when attacking or taking damage. The Ashina Taro Troop are practically raised on these fruits, which is why they all know the best time to pick them.

Persimmon

A red, ripe persimmon, ready to eat. For a time, allows one to recover Posture even when attacking or taking damage.

Ashina persimmons are particularly nutritious, perhaps because the trees grow in such pure water. Persimmons become blood, and blood becomes rice. This may be of help to one short of blood.

Sweet Rice Ball

A sweet, sticky rice ball made by Kuro.

Slowly grants medium Vitality recovery and constant Posture recovery over time.

Wolf senses it was created with feelings of resolve and a reluctance to part ways.

Such deep emotions tend to be mumbled to oneself rather than shared.

Sweet Rice Ball

Sweet, sticky rice ball made by Kuro using rice from the Child of Rejuvenation. Slowly grants medium Vitality recovery and constant Posture recovery over time.

Once when the Wolf was starving, this father wordlessly handed him a rice ball. It was astoundingly delicious.

This one is sure to taste just as good.

Fine Snow

Chilled, silver rice that spilled from the palms of the Child of Rejuvenation. Gradually recovers Vitality for a time, slightly moreso than regular rice.

The cold sweetens the rice. Rice is indeed precious. The flavor grows richer and richer, raising one's spirits higher than ever.

Rice

Rice that spilled from the palms of the Child of Rejuvenation. Gradually recovers Vitality for a time.

Even in falsehood, the power of the Dragon's Blood brings a bountiful harvest.

Rice is precious. The flavor grows richer with each bite and is sure to raise one's spirits.

Contact Medicine

Powdered medicine with poisonous effects used through the ages by Ashina shinobi.

A weak "Poison" status abnormality is inflicted upon consumption. By inflicting a weak poison on oneself, all other forms of poison become ineffective. Some shinobi also use this medicine for a specific technique. Poison is said to expand the mind.

Eel Liver

A miraculous drug capable of banishing lightning offered at the Ashina Clan altar.

Greatly reduces the amount of damage received from lightning attacks, as well as the "Shock" status abnormality. Lightning is a force of the gods. Eels, while small, are relatives of dragons.

Even a god's force can be suppressed, though probably not for long.

Pacifying Agent

Powered medicine for calming nerves, used by those who deal in unspeakable deeds.

Reduces Terror buildup and increases Terror resistance for thirty seconds.

Grave keepers, executioners, the Memorial Mob...all who keep death close keep this powder closer, adhering to a simple rule: If seized with fear, cover your rear.

Ministry Dousing Powder

Powdered medicine for treating burns, carried by Interior Ministry guards. Slightly more effective than regular dousing powder, it heals the "Burn" status, reduces Burn buildup, and reduces damage from incoming Burn attacks.

The Ministry feared Ashina, her eyes bloodshot with the waters of Rejuvenation. This powder acted as a ward for when the time came to turn flame to her walls.

Dousing Powder

Medicine for treating burns. Heals the "Burn" status abnormality and, for a time, decreases Burn buildup while increasing Burn resistance. When fire is used on the battlefield, Dousing Powder is crucial for survival.

Antidote Powder

A powerful antidote concocted by the Sunken Valley clan.

Heals the status abnormality "Poison" and, for a time, decreases Poison buildup while increasing Poison resistance.

Magnetic deposits are found in the Sunken Valley, but the place is dangerously toxic. Antidote Powder is essential for anyone attempting to mine the ore.

Academics' Red Lump

A round, red lump, found inside the body of red-eyed Dojun.

Consume to gain Red-eyes and reduce flinching from enemy attacks, but it also prohibits the use of Resurrection. Dosaku and Dojun were the quintessential master and disciple. Often when pursuing the ideal self, one need only look within.

Red Lump

A round, red lump, found inside the body of red-eyed Kotaro and Jinzaemon.

Consume to gain Red-eyes and reduce flinching from enemy attacks, but it also prohibits the use of Resurrection. The red mass will not mold nor wither, and though it does no harm, it will likely remain in the stomach even after its potency has worn off.

Red Lump

Gain Red-eyes and reduce flinching from enemy attacks. But also prohibits the use of Resurrection.

A red mass is the lingering trace of one who was unable to achieve their desires. Slightly warm to the touch. It pulsates softly.

Hidden Tooth

False tooth loaded with a secret shinobi drug, blue in color.

Can be used repeatedly.

Crush the blue nostrum between the back teeth to die as often as one pleases.

Could be useful in certain situations.

Surely an unnecessary reminder, but the first death is typically one's last.

Bite Down

Secret shinobi drug, blue in color, carried by the Nightjar Ninja.

Death by one's own hand. Some fail to realize the necessity, betraying Ashina, living out their lives no matter what... Simply crush with the back teeth to die. To think that nothing more was required.

Resurrection is not limited after use.

Bite Down

Secret shinobi drug, blue in color.

When times call for death by one's own hand, samurai turn their swords on themselves as a matter of pride, while shinobi demand a swifter means. Simply crush the candy and take the back teeth to die. Nothing more is required.

Resurrection is not limited after use.

Yashariku's Sugar

Sugar candy made in Senpou Temple, sustaining Yashariku's blessing. Halves max Vitality and Posture, while granting a large Attack Power boost.

Bite the candy and take the Yashariku stance to impart its inhuman benediction.

Forbidden at the temple, this candy was distributed far and wide in exchange for donations towards costly undying research.

Gachiin's Sugar

The High Priest of Senpou Temple gave this candy to a band of short but adept assassins. Suppresses sound and presence for a time, making the user harder to detect.

Bite the candy and take the Gachiin stance to impart its inhuman benediction.

The assassins do Senpou's dirty work. Once hired guards, now extensions of the monks' will in their quest for undeath.

Gokan's Sugar

Sugar candy made by Shinobi Hunters of Misen Temple, sustaining Gokan's blessing. Reduces Posture damage for a time. Bite the candy and take the Gokan stance to impart its inhuman benediction. Misen monks are well versed in the art of killing shinobi—an undertaking that demands a body with an unshakable core.

Ungo's Sugar

Sugar candy made in Senpou Temple, sustaining Ungo's blessing. Temporarily reduces Vitality damage from physical attacks. Bite the candy and take the Ungo stance to impart its inhuman benediction. By doing so, you endure the excess karma of man from the spirits within. Senpou monks spread this candy across Ashina in honor of her military heroes.

Ako's Sugar

Sugar candy made in Senpou Temple, sustaining Ako's blessing. Boosts Attack Power for a time. Bite the candy and take the Ako stance to impart its inhuman benediction. The spirits embody excess karma. One must bite down hard on the candy and endure what has been brought to pass.

Divine Grass

A secret medicine that fully restores Vitality and cures all status abnormalities. One small part of Ashina is exceedingly old. The ancient soil, rocks, and water that pervaded the land are said to have attracted the attention of the gods. The doctor Dogen studied the plants in this ancient place, resulting in the recipe for this special medicine.

Yashariku's Spiritfall
Fallen, headless spirit of Yashariku. Briefly sacrifice Vitality and Posture while gaining a large Attack Power boost. Consume Spirit Emblems to use repeatedly.
Headless are the ruined form of corrupted heroes who once fought for their country. This brave soul's twin was lost in utero. He may not have fallen to the palace nobles had his sibling been at his side...

Gachiin's Spiritfall
Fallen, headless spirit of Gachiin. Suppresses sound and presence, making the user harder to detect. Consume Spirit Emblems to use repeatedly.
Headless are the ruined form of corrupted heroes who once fought for their country. "I'm falling to pieces," said the man to himself, drifting deep into the forest.

Gokan's Spiritfall
Fallen, headless spirit of Gokan. Reduces Posture damage taken for a time. Consume Spirit Emblems to use repeatedly.
Headless are the ruined form of corrupted heroes who once fought for their country. Dedicated burial mounds quietly appease the spirits with severed heads, though none call upon them for long.

Ungo's Spiritfall
Fallen, headless spirit of Ungo that reduces Vitality damage taken from physical attacks. Consume Spirit Emblems to use repeatedly.
Headless are the ruined form of corrupted heroes who once fought for their country. This warrior lost his mind in defense of the state. His attempted mutiny was met with a swift beheading, and the lifeless body sunk to the bottom of the moat.

Ako's Spiritfall
Fallen, headless spirit of Ako that increases Vitality and Posture damage for a time. Consume Spirit Emblems to use repeatedly.
Headless are the ruined form of corrupted heroes who once fought for their country. Seize the power of an inhuman spirit by laying it to rest but risk going quite mad unless something is offered in return.

Divine Confetti
Confetti imbued with a divine blessing made for driving away apparitions.
The paper is made ceremoniously, whereby pulp is spread thin using water from the exalted Fountainhead. As the gods bless the waters, so too will the confetti bless one who basks in its touch, allowing attacks to connect with apparition-type enemies.

Snap Seed
Fumewort seeds that make a loud noise if you snap them. Useful for breaking the effect of illusion techniques. If an illusion occurs, it is because someone created it. To crush the phantoms and return to reality, one must defeat the creator of the illusion. Snap seeds can be of great help in that regard.

Oil
Plain oil. When the jar breaks, the oil covers everything nearby. Enemies covered in oil are more vulnerable to the "Burn" status abnormality.

Fistful of Ash
Ash gripped into a hardened clump. Throw it at an enemy to temporarily distract them. In Ashina, the snow falls thick, and thus, the hearth runs thick with ash.

Ceramic Shard
A piece of pottery that breaks with a satisfying crack when thrown.
Throw it at an enemy to draw their attention. Throwing and smashing such pieces made for a popular sport amongst Ashina boys. Even after growing up, they remember the old games well.

Mibu Pilgrimage Balloon
Mibu balloon made in the year of the Dragonspring pilgrimage, sealed with a prayer for healthy upbringing. Burst the white Mibu balloon while clasping one's hands in prayer, Those splashed with the water will enjoy increased gains of all sorts for a time. On it is crudely scrawled: "To Tenkichi, from Badger."

Mibu Balloon of Spirit
A Mibu balloon filled with Fountainhead water, imbued with a blessing of sympathy. If one pops this black and white balloon and prays, those its water splashes upon will have a higher chance of obtaining Spirit Emblems for a period of time. This balloon expresses mourning for the dearly departed. Red and white pinwheels are offered in fond remembrance.

Mibu Possession Balloon
A Mibu balloon filled with Fountainhead water, imbued with a blessing of fortune. If one pops this vibrant-green Mibu balloon and prays, those its water splashes upon will have a higher chance of obtaining items. "Mibu" means "aquatic life," or "life born of the water." The Ashina consider the Fountainhead water itself to be worthy of worship.

Mibu Balloon of Soul
A Mibu balloon filled with Fountainhead water, imbued with a blessing for departed souls. If one pops this sakura-pink balloon and prays, those its water splashes upon will acquire more Resurrective Power for a time. The oldest of the Mibu balloons, Mibu priests are known to pop them as an offering of peace to the departed.

Mibu Balloon of Wealth
A Mibu balloon filled with Fountainhead water, imbued with a blessing of wealth. If one pops the golden Mibu balloon and prays, those its water splashes upon will acquire more coin for a period of time. "Mibu" means "aquatic life," or "life born of the water." The Ashina consider the Fountainhead water itself to be worthy of worship.

Jinza's *Jizo* Statue
Buddha effigy bound in light-pink cloth. Raise in prayer between one's palms to restore a node of Resurrective Power.
To enswathe a *jizo* statue is to express feelings of parental love.
"Lord Sakuza... Please take this cloth and use it to bundle this little one, so that he may live on in peace."

Bundled *Jizo* Statue
Small Buddha effigy bound in red cloth. Raise in prayer between one's palms to restore a node of Resurrective Power.
To enswathe a *jizo* statue is to express feelings of parental love. The bundle of cloth is to at least ensure that the little one goes on in peace.

Bulging Coin Purse
A purse almost overflowing with *sen*. It can be used to acquire the *sen* inside. Hefty enough to bring something resembling a grin to a Wolf's face. The *sen* in this purse is not lost upon death.

Heavy Coin Purse
A purse filled with a large amount of *sen*. It can be used to acquire the *sen* inside. Its weight is very promising indeed. The *sen* in this purse is not lost upon death.

Light Coin Purse
A purse filled with a small amount of *sen*. It can be used to acquire the *sen* inside. Has a somewhat satisfying weight to it. The *sen* in this purse is not lost upon death.

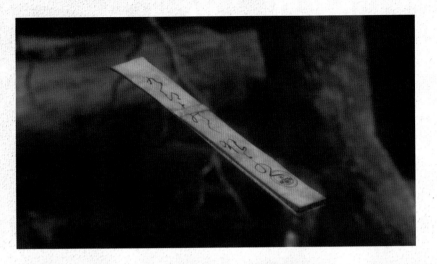

Dragon's Blood Droplet
An item that is rarely dropped by a Divine Heir of the Dragon's Heritage.
Using it will slightly increase Resurrective Power. Restore the power of life to those who have been drained of it by offering this drop to the Sculptor's Idol with the Recovery Charm in hand.
In turn, all afflicted with Dragonrot will be healed. The incessant coughing must cease.

LETTERS AND TEXTS

Page's Diary
An old diary entry written by Takeru's page.
"Lord Takeru held his arm over the incense burner, and attempted to cut it with a sword. But incredibly, his wound healed instantly, and not a drop of blood was shed.
Lady Tomoe said, 'Without it, your blood cannot be spilled.'
What could she be referring to, I wonder?"

Okami's Ancient Text
An old note left by the Okami clan, who sought to reach the divine realm.
"A fragrant stone, enshrined in a village within the depths of Ashina. One must throw oneself for it to be found.
With this, the Fountainhead Fragrance is complete. Let us depart now, to the divine realm."

Fragrant Flower Note
A note from Kuro, written by Takeru, former Heir of the Dragon's Heritage.
"It is said that relatives of the Tomoe once gathered the Fountainhead Fragrance and arrived at the palace.
You may find a key where the waters of rejuvenation converge in a deep pool. A white and deeply fragrant flower..."

Immortal Severance Text
A book from Kuro on the art of severing ties with the Dragon's Heritage. It looks old. The binding is torn, and several pages are missing.
"Herein describes the means to perform the Rite of Immortal Severance. Beyond the Fountainhead Palace, locate the Sanctuary and imbibe the tears of the holy dragon of the divine realm."

Immortal Severance Scrap
Part of the Book of Immortal Severance, left behind by Takeru.
"With Mortal Blade in hand, my blood may be shed. With my blood, the aroma will be complete.
The divine realm will be in reach.
Immortal Severance will be at hand.
I must ask Tomoe to assist with the beheading..."

Holy Chapter: Dragon's Return
Sacred passage on a path to enlightenment.
"Undying, I pray for the Dragon's return. Undying, lo, let us wait an age; for the Divine Heir to assimilate the cold dragon tears; for the cradle to consume the pair of serpentine fruits.
Let the cradle endure, giving Him shelter; granting His return to the west."

Holy Chapter: Infested
A passage describing a journey to enlightenment.
"For an age, I have been blessed by the worm. To be undying is to walk the eternal path to enlightenment, thus I must become enlightened to understand why I cannot die. It is said the holy dragon's origins were in the west. So I wonder, how did the worm come to be bestowed upon me?"

Black Scroll
An old text describing a black Mortal Blade.
"In addition to the red Mortal Blade, there exists one that is black in color.
The blade's name is "Open Gate," and it is said to hold the power to open a gate to the underworld. It is through this power that it creates life. I beseech you, 'make offerings for the Dragon's Blood...'"

Isshin's Letter
A note by Isshin in the watchtower. Perhaps Emma knows his current whereabouts.
"Dear Emma,
The Ashina Castle Gate has grown loud with the sound of scurrying. The Tengu will see to the rats, worry not.
Isshin"

Ornamental Letter
A letter thrown into a well.
"Kuro's Wolf,
Your destiny awaits you at the Moon-View Tower. Escape from the well and find the tower bathed in moonlight.
Even without a blade, you can reach it. Stay silent. Stay vigilant."

Tomoe's Note
A note written in Tomoe's soft handwriting.
"Lord Takeru's coughs are worsening still; returning to the divine realm is hopeless, and I wish only to sever the Dragon's Heritage and restore his humanity.
Restoration requires the Everblossom and Mortal Blade, and yet I cannot acquire the latter. It was hidden by the High Priest of Senpou Temple, who has no desire to sever the immortal ties..."

Rotting Prisoner's Note
A note left by a dead and rotting man in the Abandoned Dungeon.
"Supposedly, the fragrant stone is enshrined in a village in the Ashina Depths. But how to interpret 'throw oneself'? This is as far as that old Okami tome could take me. But did they truly reach the Fountainhead Palace? I'd like to know. but it seems I never will. Kotaro...forgive me..."

Surgeon's Stained Letter
A tattered, blood-covered note written by Dosaku, the surgeon in the Abandoned Dungeon.
"At the bottom of the Mibu Village pond, you will find a sakura carp.
You will know it from its red eyes,
Which are said to never rot, I require those red eyes.
Dosaku"

Surgeon's Bloody Letter
A worn and bloodstained letter from Dosaku, the surgeon in the Abandoned Dungeon:
"Required: 1 tough man. Preferably a strong samurai, or a young, large soldier such as a member of the Taro Troop.
Must be delivered unharmed.
Dosaku"

Dosaku's Note
An old note left by the surgeon Dosaku:
"My disciples have abandoned me for Dogen. Unwilling to dirty their own hands, they all left me for that hypocritical quack. Dojun! My last disciple! Even if I die, the research must continue. Finish the procedure, for Ashina's sake!
Dosaku"

Rat Description
A description of the "rats" that have snuck into Ashina. Speak to the Tengu again once the rats are dealt with.
"The rats:
- Assassins from Senpou Temple.
- Short stature, wear bamboo hats.
- A number of rats are lurking about.
- Last seen around Ashina Castle Gate."

Herb Catalogue Scrap
A page torn from the Ashina Herb Catalogue, a compendium of flowers and herbs.
"The 'Snap Seed' naturally grows in ravines and deep valleys.
According to denizens of the Sunken Valley, such places are appropriate for offering oneself in marriage to the Great Serpent.
If one wishes to become a bride, they must enter the belly of the Serpent in the valley."

Three-Story Pagoda Memo
Memo describing the three-story pagoda.
"It is said a precious treasure was once held within the Hirata Estate pagoda; a three-fold tower stood upon a precipice along a slope lined with bamboo groves.
Seems the treasure is related to shinobi techniques. The truth of it escapes me, but they called it 'blessed mist'..."

Valley Apparitions Memo
A note about apparitions in the sunken Valley.
"Apparitions have been sighted in the Guardian Ape of the Sunken Valley's old den. Angry spirits, with many faces. The Guardian Ape's old den can be found at the bottom of the Sunken Valley, not far from the Forest of Mist.
Also, some reported they could hear the sound of a woman crying in the distance..."

Sabimaru Memo
A memo detailing the whereabouts of a *kodachi* short sword known as Sabimaru.
"The ancient kodachi Sabimaru can be found within Ashina Castle, enshrined in the bottom floor of the keep. Sabimaru was wielded in wars of old and is a national treasure of Ashina.
Supposedly, the blade's poisonous blue rust could drive off even the inhuman Okami warrior women."

Nightjar Beacon Memo
A note on smoke signals used by Ashina shinobi, the Grey Nightjars.
"Pale-pink smoke signals are placed along the rooftops of Ashina Castle.
These signals guide the Nightjar.
The ashen-feathered flock are surely the only ones able to follow such a trail."

Flame Barrel Memo
A tattered note written by Anayama. Seems to be from some years ago.
"Lucrative info #36.
When we broke into the Hirata Estate, we found a barrel that spewed flame. The boys lit a roaring bonfire with it and made merry with the drink. Must have been a shinobi's tool."

Mushin Esoteric Text
A unique text of the legendary Ashina Mushin Compound Style.
Young Isshin would stop at nothing in his lust for power, and this single-minded search for strength ended in him taking Ashina for his own. This is the result of combining techniques from the styles he encountered. This drive defined Isshin's achievements, and as such, this text will never be finished.

Senpou Esoteric Text
A book of secrets that grants the ability to learn "Senpou Style" skills.
Those of the Senpou Temple mastered martial arts in the pursuit of virtue. They considered strong fists and strict discipline essential against Buddha's enemies. However, Senpou Temple was seized by an obsession for the Undying, which corrupted their teachings and style.

Ashina Esoteric Text
A compendium of the Ashina Sword Style. Allows one to learn "Ashina Style" skills.
The text reads like a history of Isshin Ashina's battles; when young, Isshin fought desperately time and time again, polishing his technique in the blood of his enemies. He consolidated his learnings under the "Ashina Style" name for the sake of his clan's dominance.

Prosthetic Esoteric Text
A book of secrets that details a variety of techniques for use with Shinobi Prosthetics. Grants the ability to learn "Prosthetic Style" skills.
Written by a man who abandoned the path of the shinobi, but could not bring himself to discard his painstaking research.
He never expected to pass these on to anyone else.

Shinobi Esoteric Text
A book of secrets that details a variety of techniques employed by shinobi. Grants the ability to learn "Shinobi Style" skills.
Within this text are the innermost secrets of the Shinobi Arts, such as attacks performed in the air and hiding one's body to avoid detection. Such moves could never be practiced by samurai.

Floating Passage Text
Compendium on the Combat Art, "Floating Passage." Skill unlocked upon acquiring this item.
"Unleash attacks in a flowing, dancelike form, overwhelming enemies in a furor of graceful aggression. This technique belongs to the Ashina sword school, though it has been deemed heretical due to its foreign origin."

Antiair Deathblow Text
Compendium on the shinobi Martial Art, "Antiair Deathblow." Skill unlocked upon acquiring this item.
"A technique which serves the shinobi who is not bound by the earth in battle.
Leap toward an opponent who has exposed himself in midair and strike, killing him before he hits the ground."

Father's Bell Charm
A bell charm previously owned by the Owl.
The Owl held this bell for a long time. Offering it at the Dilapidated Temple may result in seeing a different memory than before. There's no way of knowing why this protective bell exists. Perhaps the Owl kept it for himself, or perhaps he meant to give it to someone...

Young Lord's Bell Charm
A bell charm received from an old woman, who asked that it be offered to Buddha.
Bell charms protect their holders through Buddha's divine protection. If one finds themselves the owner of another's bell charm, offering it to Buddha on their behalf is a common courtesy. The Sculptor at the Dilapidated Temple can advise on how it should be offered.

Dragonrot Blood Sample
Blood sample of a Dragonrot victim. Contains stagnated blood.
Emma can use this to find a cure for Dragonrot.

Recovery Charm
A Dragonrot Recovery Charm created by Emma.
With this charm, one can offer a Dragon's Blood Droplet at a Sculptor's Idol to restore all afflicted with Dragonrot back to health.
The charm contains a Dragonrot victim's blood, which Emma managed to purify and solidify into a bloodstone.

Kuro's Charm
Charm received from Kuro.
Placed on the Wolf's person in secret, after he lost his life in the Hirata Estate and gained the power of Resurrection.
The charm has protected the Wolf well, tempering his ordeals. To part with it would mean facing a path of hardship beyond that endured thus far.

Key Items

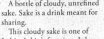

Unrefined Sake
A bottle of cloudy, unrefined sake. Sake is a drink meant for sharing.

This cloudy sake is one of Isshin Ashin's favorites. It has a rich, full-bodied flavor.

On the other hand, it has a reputation for getting one too drunk, too quickly.

Ashina Sake
A bottle of Ashina-brewed sake. Sake is a drink meant for sharing.

While it does not contain water from the Fountainhead, it is made from the purest of waters, and is a drink beloved by the people of Ashina.

Gun Fort Shrine Key
The key to a shrine deep within the gun fort. The gate behind the shrine's idol is made to be opened. The Sunken Valley clan will shoot any stranger who approaches, and the Snake Eyes' guns are particularly feared.

This elite group of women are descendants of the ancient Okami clan. Their especially sharp eyes allow them to snipe victims at a great range.

Hidden Temple Key
The key to the Hidden Temple in the Hirata Estate, given by the Owl.

The secret temple is located in the very back of the Hirata Estate.

"Two,
The Lord is absolute.
Defend him with your life.
If he is taken, bring him back at any cost."

Gatehouse Key
The key to a samurai gatehouse located in the Ashina Reservoir, not far from the well the Wolf was kept in.

Here, Gyoubu Masataka Oniwa is respectfully guarded by Ashina samurai. The Broken Horn is the spear blade once wielded by Gyoubu the Demon. It's said that no prey can escape Gyoubu's horn.

It pulls enemies in and is even capable of stripping an enemy's armor.

Secret Passage Key
The key to the secret passage that leads out of Ashina Castle.

The secret passage can be found at the end of the moat in the Ashina Reservoir, not far from the Moon-View Tower.

Kuro has escaped the castle through this passage, and the Wolf looks to join him there.

Promissory Note
An Ashina trade promissory note. Matabei Anayama's last piece of product.

Discounts the cost of items when purchasing from merchants.

A *sen* saved is a *sen* earned. And so long as one draws breath, business will continue.

Rice for Kuro
Rice that has spilled forth from the hand of the Divine Child of Rejuvenation. Intended to be a gift for Kuro.

"Rice is precious. I want nothing more than for the Divine Heir of the Dragon's Heritage to get better."

Kuro would likely be pleased to receive it.

White Pinwheel
A small pinwheel made of white paper. Found below a cliff at Mount Kongo.

Perhaps it was carried there by the wind.

It is simply a single, pure white pinwheel. Only the child is right here.

Red and White Pinwheel
A small pinwheel made of red and white paper. Found about halfway up Mount Kongo.

The red and white pinwheels simply spin round and round. Everyone is right here.

Dragonspring Sake
A bottle of crystal-clear sake. Sake is a drink meant for sharing.

A top-shelf sake brewed by the Ashina brewmaster with water from the Dragonspring.

The pure water extracts every last bit of flavor from Ashina's finest rice. There are no words that can do the flavor justice. To understand, one must taste it for themselves.

Monkey Booze
Alcohol created by dew pooled in a hollow tree.

Fruits hidden by monkeys in tree hollows can sometimes ferment and turn into sake with a bit of luck.

While it's known for its brutally harsh flavor, some find this acquired taste irresistible.

Truly Precious Bait
This is truly precious bait. If bait has hair, you know it's something truly special.

The Fountainhead Palace noble in the pot is obsessed with becoming one with the "master."

"Present this bait to the master, the Great Colored Carp. Offer it earnestly, but quietly, so no one knows..."

Truly Precious Bait
This is truly precious bait. If bait has hair, you know it's something truly special.

The Hirata noble in the pot is obsessed with thoughts of becoming a "master."

"He who receives the scales of the carp becomes closer to a carp himself... I bestow unto you my secret treasure."

Precious Bait
This is precious bait. The texture is slimy, and something resembling horns seem to jut out of it. Just the kind of bait the "master" loves.

"Ring the bell, drop the bait."

Water of the Palace
A cup filled with divine waters, a drink popular with nobles of the palace.

When a wedding procession arrives at the Fountainhead palace, this is the drink they are greeted with.

"The nectar of the palace nobles.
Go ahead, drink to your heart's content."

Red Carp Eyes
It has two red eyes.

Carp with only eyes that are red cannot become "masters."

Though they're considered incomplete creatures that lack the ideal number of scales, their eyes are said to be everlasting.

The researcher Dojun in the Abandoned Dungeon wants these eyes to improve his "procedure."

Dragon's Tally Board
A tally board carved from a large piece of jade. Possessing this increases the stocks that can be purchased in merchants' shops.

Such a tally board is highly prized by the merchant class. Old custom dictates that those of dragon rank are recognized as supreme merchants by the imperial palace, and should be given the best possible treatment.

Aromatic Branch
Dried aromatic wood from the Everblossom. Plucked by the Wolf's father.

The Everblossom is a sakura tree and, as such, is ripe with nostalgia. Takeru would likely gaze upon this branch when once it bloomed, reminded of home.

One of the incense ingredients sought by the Divine Heir for Immortal Severance.

Shelter Stone
A stone found on an altar deep within the village of the water-dwellers. Stones will sometimes appear in the bodies of those who have long drank from the Fountainhead waters.

"Step into the marital shrine and offer the fragrant, auspicious stone."

One of the incense ingredients sought by the Divine Heir for Immortal Severance.

Lotus of the Palace
A white lotus flower found blooming in the depths of the Sunken Valley, where the Fountainhead waters pool deeply.

The flower's aroma attracts female apes. Thus, the Guardian Ape carefully tended to it, so as to offer it to his bride. One of the incense ingredients sought by the Divine Heir for Immortal Severance.

Bell Demon
A demonic spirit sealed within the Iron Bell of Senpou Temple.

Possesses those who ring the bell, strengthening enemies around them.

The Bell Demon confers hardship, but perhaps also slightly better spoils.

Using this item has no particular effect aside from causing the demon to leave.

Treasure Carp Scale
A sparking scale from a Treasure Carp.

To the average person, it is just a beautiful scale. But there are some who exalt a certain "master," who consider these scales among the most precious things in the world. For this reason, collecting them could be worthwhile.

Great White Whisker
A priceless whisker taken from the Great Colored Carp.

While the Great Colored Carp is naturally immortal, if killed, its whiskers can be plucked.

The sound of the whisker being removed is surely music to the ears of certain people. Some would feel relief at the sound of their mission being completed—others, the joy of having their heart's desire granted.

Frozen Tears

Tears that were shed by the Divine Child of Rejuvenation once she became the cradle. They are but frozen drops.

By having Kuro drink both the Dragon Tears and Frozen Tears, the Cradling ritual can be performed. Cold Dragon Tears are just that.

Divine Dragon's Tears

Tears received from the Divine Dragon. The gracious gift of tears can only be granted by the Mortal Blade.

The body of the Divine Dragon is eternal, and its tears, once shed, will maintain their form and moisture in perpetuity. Should one of the Dragon's Heritage partake of the dragon's tears, Immortal Severance will be reified.

Dried Serpent Viscera

A dried, persimmon-like heart of a Great Serpent. The Great Serpent is a god of the land, and the heart is believed to be where one's spirit resides. While it looks much like a persimmon, in fact, this is the red viscera of a god.

Apparently, denizens of the Sunken Valley worship the organs, believing they represent the deity itself.

Fresh Serpent Viscera

The persimmon-like heart of a Great Serpent.

The Great Serpent is considered to be a god of the land, and the heart is believed to be where one's spirit resides. While its shape bears similarity to a persimmon, in fact, this is the red viscera of a god. It is safe to assume that eating it would be poisonous to one's health.

Aromatic Flower

Flowers of the Everblossom that bloomed in an old memory. Grafted by Takeru, who took the branch from the divine realm as a parting relic.

One who seeks Purification may impart the Dragon Tears and these flowers to the Divine Heir of the Dragon's Heritage, thus severing the shackles that bind the immortal bearer of Dragon's Blood.

Charmed One

The coughing and wheezing sounds of a man who is enamored with a beautiful melody.

Lost Child

The coughing and wheezing sounds of one who seems to be a lost child in a large body.

Black Hat

The coughing and wheezing comes from a man who wants nothing more than to return to an abandoned place.

Newcomer

The coughing and wheezing comes from one who travels frequently, looking to expand his business.

Sculptor

The man who coughs zealously sculpts statues of Buddha to avoid being consumed by the building flames.

ROT ESSENCE

Somewhere, a pained cough rings out continuously.

Owning this item reduces one's chances of receiving Unseen Aid.

Faithful One

The coughing and wheezing sounds of an old woman of great faith. Keeping one's faith even when driven mad allows one to see certain things. Thank heavens...

Timid Maid

The coughing and wheezing sounds of an old woman deeply worried about her beloved master.

Thirsty One

The coughing and wheezing sounds of a man who is both frightened and thirsty.

Fine Son

The coughing and wheezing sounds of a man thinking only of his sick mother.

Surgeons

The coughing and wheezing are coming from a deeply troubled pair of researchers who are nonetheless tireless in their work.

Info Broker

The coughing and wheezing sounds of a man who makes his living dealing in information, yet cannot remove himself from compassion.

Drunk Mob

The coughing and wheezing sounds of a drunk who has forgotten the sincerity of offerings, yet offers them regardless.

Pious Mob

The coughing and wheezing sounds of a man who holds memorials for the dead in a place where Buddha has been forgotten.

Toxic Mob

He who coughs finds himself near poisonous pools. He works to make offerings to those Buddha cannot save.

Jail Mob

The man who coughs seems to be one who frequently sees those gruesomely abandoned. Even so, he continues to make offerings to the dead.

Wartorn Mob

The coughing and wheezing sounds of one who is near death. The man who coughs has witnessed endless battles, making offerings to the dead in the battlefield outside the Ashina Castle Gate.

Crow Mob

The coughing and wheezing sounds of a man who takes great pride in memorializing the dead. He holds service somewhere in the Ashina Outskirts.

SHINOBI ARTS

Shadowrush
Unleash a long-range, powerful thrust, then use the impaled opponent as a platform to vault into the skies. Be as an owl on the hunt and return to the skies after stabbing your prey. Spirit Emblems are consumed when leaping.

Whirlwind Slash
A spinning attack that can hit several enemies at once. The sharp cut combined with the force of the spin can strike multiple foes and deal damage even when guarded. When surrounded by enemies, this shinobi technique can cut open a path to victory.

COMBAT ARTS

Unique skills, different from your regular attacks, are called Combat Arts. There are a variety of schools, such as the way of the shinobi, the path of the sword, and even militant fists...

"Whether you make use of them or not is up to you. Shinobi aren't the only ones with their own fighting techniques."

Just as the Sculptor says, what you choose to master is up to you. The more you learn, the closer you get to obtaining secret techniques.

PROSTHETIC ARTS

Nightjar Slash Reversal
Performs a spinning leap attack that can quickly close or create distance from foes. This technique allows one to decide which direction to rotate in when performing Nightjar Slash. Making use of both directions makes this both an offensive and a defensive skill.

Nightjar Slash
A spinning leap attack that can quickly close or create distance from foes. A technique of the Nightjar clan, the shinobi who serve Ashina.

The Nightjar use the weight of their massive shuriken to add force to the blow. The Shinobi Prosthetic is made of heavy steel and can be used in a similar capacity.

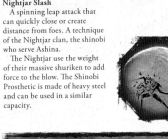

ASHINA ARTS

Ashina Cross
From a sheathed stance, draw the blade at a high speed. Costs Spirit Emblems to use. Hold the stance to intercept at will. A secret technique of the Ashina style, devoted to the mastery of a swift kill. Draws a cruciform cut in the blink of an eye—so fast, it could sever the arm of Shura, or so boasts Isshin Ashina.

Ichimonji: Double
Adds a follow-up overhead sword strike to Ichimonji. Deals high Posture damage and also recovers one's own Posture with a strong, forward step. The follow-up attack is especially useful for preventing enemy counterattacks. Ashina's Ichimonji is perfected with this follow-up strike.

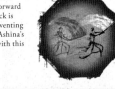

Ichimonji
Ichimonji delivers a heavy, one-hit, overhead sword strike. Deals high Posture damage and also recovers one's own Posture with a strong, forward step. Single-minded mastery of this technique is the heart of the Ashina style's strength. Once mastered, it can likely be improved.

MUSHIN ARTS

Empowered Mortal Blade
A secret technique using the Mortal Blade. Costs Spirit Emblems to use. By focusing one's mind before unsheathing the Mortal Blade, one can draw additional power, resulting in a longer-ranged, more powerful slash attack. Draw the sword that cannot be drawn, and unleash its devastation.

Spiral Cloud Passage
A sword technique that unleashes powerful shockwaves. Costs Spirit Emblems to use. Its namesake comes from a large eddy of distant clouds forming near the headwaters; the Fountainhead Spiral. Tomoe would watch her young master as he gazed longingly at the coiling clouds. The sight meant everything to her.

Shadowfall
An evolution of Shadowrush, this is a secret technique of the Ashina Mushin Compound Style. After leaping into the skies with Shadowrush, it allows one to perform a spinning sword attack as they descend. Pierce, fly, and then dive back down. Jumping off the enemy costs Spirit Emblems.

Senpou Leaping Kicks

Acquires the "Senpou Leaping Kick" Combat Art, where repeated attacks begin with a leaping kick. A combined antiair counter and sweep attack counter, followed up with a combination of kicks. A technique refined by the recluses of Senpou. According to their practices, mastery of the Leaping Kick proves one has attained true enlightenment.

Praying Strikes

Unleash a flurry of quick attacks, inflicting damage while preventing counterattack. Then use a heavier blow using one's entire body to complete the combination. The Senpou monks also used this technique as a way to purge themselves of worldly desires. However...

NINJUTSU SKILLS

Bloodsmoke Ninjutsu

Ninjutsu technique that turns the spraying blood of a victim to smoke. Costs Spirit Emblems to use. Activated after a Backstab Deathblow.

The smokescreen allows one to retake the element of surprise. Life-and-death struggle defines a shinobi, for whom a kill is a source of strength.

High Monk

The secret technique of the Senpou Style, this adds sword slashes and additional kicks to the Senpou Leaping Kicks. The technique has no form, and the attacks differ from person to person. For Wolf, it's only natural that he'd rely on Kusabimaru when performing the technique.

Praying Strikes - Exorcism

Using successive elbow and arm strikes, unleash a flurry of quick attacks that inflict damage while preventing counterattack. The strikes are both a martial art and a form of prayer. "Without strength, one cannot defeat the enemies of Buddha..."

MORE

Puppeteer Ninjutsu

Ninjutsu technique that manipulates the victim like a puppet. Costs Spirit Emblems to use. Activated after a Backstab Deathblow.

This technique temporarily forces one who should have fled this realm to remain. A puppet moves on behalf of its master, but its strings are destined to snap.

Mortal Draw

A Combat Art using the Mortal Blade. Costs Spirit Emblems to use.

With the flash of a sword, the blade slashes through enemies, leaving a reddish-black, noxious mist. The seeping mist extends the range of the blade.

A technique using the blade that cannot be drawn is a feat only the oathbound of the Divine Heir could achieve.

Floating Passage

Unleashes repeated attacks, overwhelming enemies with flowing, dance-like movements. While an Ashina Combat Art, it was taught by an outsider and, as such, is considered heretical. The master of this technique crossed the Floating Passage and descended to Ashina. Her name was Tomoe.

Bestowal Ninjutsu

Ninjutsu technique that wreathes a blade in the victim's blood, extending its reach. Costs Spirit Emblems to use. Activated after a Backstab Deathblow. The Wolf discovered this technique upon beheading a foe with the Mortal Blade, forming a cursed sword from spilled blood. Though it bears likeness to the Mortal Blade, it cannot kill the undying.

One Mind

A Combat Art that unleashes a storm of attacks from the sheathed stance—so fast, the blade is nigh invisible. Costs Spirit Emblems to use. One must focus their soul on the release of the blade—nothing else. Through that focus, the strikes achieve a godlike speed. Only one as honed as the aging Isshin Ashina could perform this technique.

Dragon Flash

Combat Art that performs a high-speed cut from a sheathed stance. Charge to send out shockwaves. Costs Spirit Emblems to use. In his younger years, Isshin was a devil with the sword, spending his days in pursuit of life-and-death combat. He often ruminated on how a cut should be made, but his blade always moved first.

Run and Slide

Allows one to slide into a crouched position while sprinting. Sprint through an area and slide into cover or otherwise out of view. This maneuver easily deceives an enemy's eyes.

Midair Deflection

Allows one to guard against or deflect enemy attacks in midair. Guns and other projectile weapons deal additional damage to airborne targets, and this technique can serve to prevent that damage. A shinobi is not shot down so easily.

Mikiri Counter

Enables one to counter enemy thrust attacks by stomping down on an enemy's weapon, dealing a large amount of damage to their Posture. It is nearly impossible to perceive the speed of a thrust, but not for the sharp eyes of a shinobi.

Grappling Hook Attack

Uses the Grappling Hook to launch oneself at an enemy, using that momentum to perform a rolling sword attack. The Shinobi Prosthetic is the perfect tool for combining movement and attack into one, ensuring no movement is wasted.

Vault Over

A Shinobi Martial Art that allows one to leap over and behind a Posture-broken enemy. This Martial Arts technique allows the use of backstab Deathblows in the middle of battle, even without using stealth.

Midair Combat Arts

Allows one to perform Combat Arts while in midair. Allows one to use combat arts after jumping close to an enemy, or immediately after jumping over a sweep attack.

Chasing Slice

A Shinobi Combat Art that allows one to perform a forward-dashing sword slice after using certain Prosthetic Tools, allowing one to close distance on enemies instantly.

Applicable Prosthetic Tools: Loaded Shuriken, Shinobi Firecracker, Loaded Spear.

Antiair Deathblow

A technique designed to stop cold any enemies that leap high in the air. Allows one to exploit an enemy's vulnerability in the air by jumping toward them and performing a sudden Deathblow. The perfect skill for shinobi looking to turn the tables on airborne enemies.

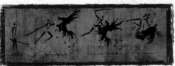

Mid-air Prosthetic Tool

Enables the use of Prosthetic Tools while in midair. The Shinobi Prosthetic is heavy as it is made from iron machinery. Despite that, it can be used in the air thanks to the techniques of its creator, Dogen, and the training of its owner.

Living Force

Allows one to perform a follow-up attack with certain Tools that imbues the sword with the Tool's effect. The Sculptor retired the Shinobi Prosthetic after developing this technique. He'd gone too far, killed too many. The flames of hatred had begun to manifest...

Applicable Prosthetic Tools: Flame Vent, Divine Abduction.

Projected Force

After using certain Prosthetic Tools, this allows one to draw the power of that Tool into the sword and release it in a forward direction. The specific attack changes depending on the tool used.

Applicable Prosthetic Tools: Loaded Umbrella, Finger Whistle.

Fang and Blade

After using certain Prosthetic Tools, this move allows one to attack with the Tool and sword simultaneously, or it provides a follow-up attack for the Tool.

Applicable Prosthetic Tools: Loaded Axe, Loaded Spear, Mist Raven.

Ascending Carp

A Latent Skill that increases the damage inflicted to Posture upon performing a successful Deflection. The Ashina Style is deeply rooted in the flow of the Fountainhead waters. They believe the act of successfully deflecting a blade is akin to a carp ascending a waterfall.

Shinobi Eyes

Increases the damage inflicted to Posture upon executing a successful Mikiri Counter. A shinobi's eyes do not follow the blade without anticipating its movements. Remaining composed even when fearful of its sharp edge is the key to victory.

Suppress Sound

A Latent Skill that suppresses movement noise by inhibiting an enemy's ability to hear it. Moving in silence is part of what defines a shinobi.

Suppress Presence

A Latent Skill that reduces an enemy's ability to perceive those who are in stealth. Removing one's presence is part of what defines a shinobi.

LATENT SKILLS

Breath of Life

Recovers Vitality upon performing a successful Deathblow. Deathblows provide shinobi with an opportunity to breathe.

Breath of Life: Light

A shinobi can calm the body and mind through measured breathing, even while killing. Doing so allows one to continue killing unabated.

Breath of Life: Shadow

Experiencing battles with powerful opponents further deepens this moment of respite.

Flowing Water

Reduces the amount of damage to Posture when attacked by an enemy with a sword. Much like the flowing waters known by the Ashina Clan, strength should not be met with more force but instead redirected like the flowing of water.

Descending Carp

A Latent Skill that, for a few seconds after Deflection, increases damage to enemy Posture from all sources. The Ashina Style is deeply rooted in the flow of the Fountainhead waters. They believe the act of successfully deflecting a blade is akin to a carp descending a waterfall.

Most Virtuous Deed

Increases the amount of *sen* obtained from enemies and improves item drop rates. In the words of the High Priest of Senpou Temple... "One should focus only on continued deeds of virtue and forego any thoughts of attaining wealth."

Virtuous Deed

Improves the amount of *sen* obtained from enemies and Improves item drop rates. In the words of the High Priest of Senpou Temple... "One should focus only on deeds of virtue and forego thoughts of attaining wealth."

Breath of Nature

Recovers Posture upon executing a successful Deathblow.

Breath of Nature: Light

The Ashina Style also has techniques designed for fighting when greatly outnumbered. After killing an enemy, one must exhale, expelling both regret and reaffirming one's core to regain Posture.

Breath of Nature: Shadow

A shinobi must be prepared for battles in which he is outnumbered. After killing an enemy, one must exhale, expelling both regret and reaffirming one's core to regain Posture. Experiencing battles with stronger opponents further deepens this moment of exhalation.

Devotion

Increases the amount of time a Buddhist candy is effective when used. Those who demonstrate devotion are blessed with the protection of the gods for an extended period.

Emma's Medicine

Increases the healing effects of recovery items. Emma taught this technique to the Sculptor long ago.

Emma's Medicine: Potency

Memorizing the flavor will enhance its effects. However, knowing this technique doesn't make the medicine taste any better.

Emma's Medicine: Aroma

Savoring and memorizing the aroma will enhance its effects. Be warned that the medicine still smells just as bad.

Shinobi Medicine

Increases the healing effect of recovery items. The only way to learn such techniques is to be gravely injured time and time again by worthy opponents.

Shinobi Medicine Rank 1

Medicinal knowledge is vital for a shinobi's survival. Receiving wounds in battle is inevitable.

Shinobi Medicine Rank 2

Sometimes a shinobi can survive what is certain death for a lesser warrior. As such, medicinal knowledge is vital.

Shinobi Medicine Rank 3

A shinobi fights as a lone wolf, without the help of others. As such, medicinal knowledge is vital.

Mibu Breathing Technique

Allows one to dive underwater, as well as breathe underwater indefinitely. Developed by the founder of Mibu Village. "Those who seek to join the procession must master the Mibu Breathing Technique. Without it, the Divine Dragon cannot be met."

Karma

Increases the maximum number of Spirit Emblems that can be held. Spirit Emblems are manifestations of regret. Those regretful of their vile actions are haunted by many Spirit Emblems.

A Shinobi's Karma: Body

Shinobi who have killed many must bear the physical toll of those sins.

A Shinobi's Karma: Mind

Shinobi who have killed many must carry the burden of their sins in their hearts.

Sculptor's Karma: Blood

Blood splattered upon the Prosthetic turns to a permanent rust—proof of the user's burden.

Sculptor's Karma: Scars

The Prosthetic's many small cuts and scars are proof of the countless deaths it has caused.

A Beast's Karma

Perhaps this innocent beast was burdened with the karma of man. Inheriting the karma of those they've killed is also part of being shinobi.

Screen Monkeys
The Folding-Screen Monkeys guarded the Halls of Illusion and befriended the Divine Child of Rejuvenation.
The Halls of Illusion lie on the threshold betwixt life and death. Departed souls of the Divine Children drift and savvy, taking shelter in the monkeys of the temple. Such is why the Divine Child of Rejuvenation speaks of them as friends.

Genichiro
As the Code dictates, the Wolf swore vengeance on Genichiro Ashina.
Born a peasant, Genichiro Ashina was taken in by the Ashina after his mother's death. With his country on the brink of defeat, Genichiro took to heretical arts and mastered the Lightning of Tomoe. Such heresy may be the key to saving her.

Lady Butterfly
The Phantom Lady Butterfly was a seasoned practitioner of illusions.
The Phantom Lady Butterfly was appointed by the Wolf's foster father as one of his mentors in the shinobi techniques. These mentors employed strict methods. The cultivation of shinobi techniques can only be achieved in the midst of battle.

Gyoubu Oniwa
Gyoubu Masataka Oniwa was the keeper of the Ashina Castle Gate.
Gyoubu Oniwa once led a group of infamous bandits but was defeated by Isshin, who was so captivated by his show of strength that he took him in as an Ashina warrior. Oniwa would later go on to become Genichiro Ashina's most trusted retainer.

The battle memory of an extraordinary foe, lingering in the mind of the Wolf.
Commune with a Sculptor's Idol and confront memories of battle to permanently increase Attack Power.

Great Shinobi
The Great Shinobi Owl was foster father to the Wolf.
The Great Shinobi Owl's unbridled ambition was to obtain the power of the Dragon's Heritage. Now is the time to let one's true name ring out across all of Japan. It was all for the sake of ambition.

True Monk
The Corrupted Monk guarded the bridge leading to the Fountainhead Palace.
The Corrupted Monk was among the infested, standing over the Fountainhead Palace. Indeed, immortality would seem a fitting quality for eternal watcher of the palace. Her true name is Priestess Yao.

Corrupted Monk
The Corrupted Monk watched over the cave entrance, deep in Mibu Village.
The Corrupted Monk donned the mask of a fierce guardian deity. Her form was nebulous, appearing as if in a dream. What reason could there have been for guarding the Mibu Village cave entrance?

Headless Ape
The Headless Guardian Ape was a colossal beast, plagued with the power of the undying.
At one time, the Guardian Ape shared its den with a mate. But he alone became infested, while others passed away. Now, even the flowers offered in tribute to her passing have withered to dust.

Guardian Ape
The Guardian Ape was defeated, though its roar can still be heard. It is said that an infested body marks the undying...
They say that an infested body is the mark of the undying, but such a long life would surely be quite lonesome even for an ape. Perhaps the echoing roar of the Guardian Ape was in fact a solicitation of sorts.

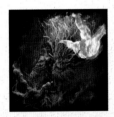

Hatred Demon
The one-armed demon prowled the battlefield, consumed by flames of deepest resentment.
A man who failed to become Shura instead became a vessel for the flames of hatred. As fate would have it, he was bound stubbornly to this world. It wasn't until he became a demon that he was finally able to depart for the next.

Saint Isshin
At his peak, Isshin Ashina devoted himself to deadly conflict in pursuit of strength. A single-minded killing machine of a man.
One who returns from the great beyond does so at the peak of their prosperity. Isshin coveted strength and all manner of techniques throughout his mortal struggle. He wished for war until his final hour, and that is precisely what he got.

Isshin Ashina
Isshin Ashina was a true master of the sword, no less so in his vale of years.
The elderly Isshin was akin to a sharpened blade. His steadily honed techniques culminated in the Ashina Style, soundly eliminating all wasted or idle movement. A master who took the spirit of his craft to its pinnacle—a true sword saint.

Divine Dragon
The Divine Dragon, ancient deity of the Everblossom.
The Divine Dragon of the Everblossom came from the west long ago, eventually making its way to this land. Some parts of Ashina are exceedingly old. Water coursing through her ancient rocks and soil allowed the Dragon to take root.

Foster Father
The foster father confronted in old memories was a man in his prime.
Owl took in the hungry cub on a whim and raised him as a shinobi. The process was so engrossing that he hoped they might enjoy a true battle to the death some day.
He got his wish, if only in an old memory.

All Ninjutsu Techniques
Acquired all Ninjutsu Techniques.

All Prosthetic Tools
Acquired all Prosthetic Tools.

Height of Technique
Acquired all skills.

Master of the Prosthetic
Upgraded all Prosthetic Tools to their limit.

Ashina Traveler
Traveled to all areas of the game.

Man Without Equal
Defeated all bosses.

Sekiro
All trophies have been unlocked.

TROPHIES AND ACHIEVEMENTS

Lazuline Upgrade
Used Lapis Lazuli to upgrade any tool to its limit.

Master of the Arts
Grasped the inner mysteries of any combat style.

Sword Saint, Isshin Ashina
Defeated Sword Saint Isshin Ashina.

Shura
Attained the "Shura" ending.

Dragon's Homecoming
Attained the "Return" ending.

Purification
Attained the "Purification" ending.

Immortal Severance
Attained the "Immortal Severance" ending.

Ultimate Healing Gourd
Fully upgraded the Healing Gourd.

Peak Physical Strength
Upgraded Vitality and Posture to their limit.

Guardian Ape Immortality Severed
Used the Mortal Blade to sever the Guardian Ape's immortality.

Guardian Ape
Defeated the Guardian Ape.

Genichiro Ashina
Defeated Genichiro Ashina.

The Phantom Lady Butterfly
Defeated Lady Butterfly.

Gyoubu Masataka Oniwa
Defeated Gyoubu Masataka Oniwa.

Resurrection
Returned from the dead using Resurrection for the first time.

Memorial Mob
Encountered a Memorial Mob merchant.

Shinobi Prosthetic
Acquired the Shinobi Prosthetic.

Revered Blade
Received the Kusabimaru from Kuro.

Great Colored Carp
Defeated the Great Colored Carp.

Great Serpent
Defeated the Great Serpent.

Demon of Hatred
Defeated the Demon of Hatred.

Isshin Ashina
Defeated Isshin Ashina.

Gracious Gift of Tears
Defeated the Divine Dragon and obtained the Divine Dragon's Tears.

Corrupted Monk
Defeated the Corrupted Monk.

Father Surpassed
Defeated Owl (Father) at the Hirata Estate.

Great Shinobi-Owl
Defeated Great Shinobi-Owl.

Folding-Screen Monkeys
Caught the Folding-Screen Monkeys.

HIRATA ESTATE

CRESTS

SENPOU TEMPLE

KUSABIMARU

FOUNTAINHEAD PALACE

DIVINE HEIR

INTERIOR MINISTRY

ASHINA

SEKIRO™
SHADOWS DIE TWICE
Official Artworks

Translation
Alexander Keller-Nelson

Lettering
Abigail Blackman

JAPANESE STAFF

Edited by Dengeki Game Books Editorial Department

Director and Editor
**Dengeki Game Books Editorial Department
(Daisuke Kihara)**

Editor
Hitomi Sakabe

Assistant
Meimi Takashima, Tsukasa Ito, Masahiko Shigeta

Designer
Tokyo Text Co., Ltd.

Cover Designer
Tokyo Text Co., Ltd.

Producer
**Dengeki Game Books Editorial Department
(Takeshi Matsumoto)**

Coordinator
**Dengeki PlayStation Editorial Department
(Akira Chigira)**

Special Thanks
FromSoftware, Inc.

SEKIRO: SHADOWS DIE TWICE Official Artworks
©2019 FromSoftware, Inc. All rights reserved. ACTIVISION is a trademark of Activision Publishing Inc.
All other trademarks and trade names are the properties of their respective owners.
First published in Japan in 2019 by KADOKAWA Game Linkage Inc., Tokyo.
English translation rights arranged with KADOKAWA Game Linkage Inc., Tokyo
through Tuttle-Mori Agency, Inc., Tokyo.

English translation © 2020 by Yen Press, LLC

Yen Press
150 West 30th Street, 19th Floor
New York, NY 10001

Visit us at yenpress.com
facebook.com/yenpress
twitter.com/yenpress
yenpress.tumblr.com
instagram.com/yenpress

First Yen Press Edition: October 2020

Yen Press is an imprint of Yen Press, LLC.
The Yen Press name and logo are trademarks of Yen Press, LLC.

The publisher is not responsible for websites (or their content) that are not owned by the publisher.

Library of Congress Control Number: 2020938733

ISBNs: 978-1-9753-1630-3 (paperback)
        978-1-9753-1631-0 (ebook)

10 9 8 7 6 5 4 3 2 1

APS

Printed in China